RIGHTSIZING THE ACADEMIC LIBRARY COLLECTION

RIGHTSIZING THE ACADEMIC LIBRARY COLLECTION

SUZANNE M. WARD

An imprint of the American Library Association

CHICAGO   2015

Suzanne M. Ward is head, collection management, at Purdue University Libraries in West Lafayette, IN. She has written and spoken extensively on patron-driven acquisitions, publishing *A Guide to Implementing and Managing Patron-Driven Acquisitions* for ALCTS in 2012 and giving presentations on this topic both nationally and internationally. Her current research interests include print retention issues and the use of e-books in academic libraries. She holds a BA from the University of California, Los Angeles, an AMLS from the University of Michigan, and an MA from Memphis State University.

Extensive effort has gone into ensuring the reliability of the information in this book; however, the publisher makes no warranty, express or implied, with respect to the material contained herein.

ISBNs
978–0-8389–1298–0 (paper)
978-0-8389-1302-4 (PDF)
978-0-8389-1303-1 (ePub)
978-0-8389-1304-8 (Kindle)

Library of Congress Cataloging-in-Publication Data
Ward, Suzanne M.
     Rightsizing the academic library collection / Suzanne M. Ward.
       pages cm
     Includes bibliographical references and index.
     ISBN 978-0-8389-1298-0 (print : alk. paper) 1. Academic libraries—Collection development—United States. 2. Collection management (Libraries)—United States. 3. Discarding of books, periodicals, etc. I. Title.
     Z675.U5W325 2015
     025.2'18770973—dc23   2014038867

Cover design by Alejandra Diaz. Images © Shutterstock, Inc.

Text composition by Dianne M. Rooney in the Chaparral, Gotham, and Bell Gothic typefaces.

♾ This paper meets the requirements of ANSI/NISO Z39.48-1992 (Permanence of Paper).

Contents

Contents

Introduction

IN 1956, MCGAW WROTE THAT THE LIBRARIANS OF HIS DAY "might conclude that we have plenty of time before we are faced with the problem of maximum size. But eventually that day will come" (McGaw 1956, 269). To say that that day is now upon us is an understatement. The stacks in many academic libraries have been bursting at the seams for years. Even when funding is available, adding new buildings, extensions, or storage facilities only postpones the inevitable. Despite the explosion in electronic resources and plummeting circulation of print resources, libraries still add thousands of items a year to their physical collections. In addition, many academic administrators are taking a close look at space on central campuses and concluding that increasingly deserted stacks space would be ideal, if cleared out, for a variety of other purposes.

We encounter the term *sustainability* more and more frequently in various aspects of our lives. In academic libraries, we know that many of our activities, both time-honored and new, are not indefinitely sustainable if based on traditional models of funding, staffing, and space. We are coming to realize that one of these activities in particular—building and maintaining local physical collections of a depth and breadth sufficient to support not only current scholars but also future ones—is not ultimately sustainable for any but a handful of the largest research libraries. Most libraries cannot afford to buy all the scholarly output that they might like; even if this were not a challenge, they cannot continue to house and maintain gigantic physical collections of material that in many cases are both rarely used locally and are widely duplicated elsewhere. Clearly the time has come (if it is not already long overdue) for academic librarians to develop a new vision about their libraries' functions and services. One aspect of implementing that new vision requires making tough decisions about *whether*, as opposed to *how*, to retain large portions of their physical collections.

The increasingly electronic library of the twenty-first century offers myriad opportunities for introducing new services and activities. However, many of these new programs require space, and not just traditionally configured space filled with shelving and study carrels. Because creating new library space is difficult to justify, library administrators must proactively seek ways to reduce the footprint of physical material, especially when hundreds or thousands of previously acquired physical items have long histories of no- or low-use, were used when acquired decades ago but are now less relevant, or are in formats that have been superseded by electronic equivalents. In the recent past, the typical solution involved building a nearby storage facility for the little-used portion of the local collection, but today an expensive storage facility may not be the right answer for many libraries. What is the obvious solution? Weeding, withdrawing, discarding, deselecting, and deaccessioning: all words that make academic librarians shudder.

This book suggests the term *rightsizing* to describe the overarching plan for shaping a library's physical collection into one that meets its users' needs. Although many libraries face the necessity of an immediate large-scale retroactive print retention project, rightsizing is much more than just a massive weeding effort. Rightsizing includes not only the initial push to remove decades of obsolete material, but also ongoing and routine evaluation activities that keep a collection fresh and relevant. Further, rightsizing usually involves awareness of regional and consortial partners' needs to conduct these same activities, and employs a variety of collaborative approaches for collectively meeting users' occasional needs for older or less-used material. Rightsizing harnesses technology to create withdrawal candidate lists that take into account many variables to ensure that a library only removes no- and low-use titles easily obtainable from resource sharing partners, and retains scarce items and items of local importance. Rightsizing employs batch processing methods to minimize title-by-title reviews and to streamline operations. Rightsizing embraces the concept of preferring electronic resources over print ones for many or most new acquisitions, so that the challenge of burgeoning, and then aging, print collections does not continue into the future. Rightsizing also advocates different approaches to some aspects of collection development, such as using patron-driven acquisitions models to add books as they are needed, rather than perpetuating the older model in which libraries buy titles that in many cases may never be used.

In the fourth edition of his book *Weeding Library Collections: Library Weeding Methods*, Slote wrote: "Every library consists of two distinguishable collections: the collection that is used, and the collection that remains unused." He called them the *core* collection and the *noncore collection*, and suggested that "once these two collections are identified, the following rule should be followed: No volume in the core collection should be considered for weeding. And, as a corollary of the above rule: All books in the noncore collection are candidates for weeding and probably should be weeded" (Slote 1997, 85).

Based on various studies that will be summarized later, most academic libraries have noncore collections of at least 40 to 50 percent. Excluding some protected classes of material (e.g., the institution's thesis collection), most of the noncore titles could be removed with "no effect whatsoever on user services. On the contrary, such straightforward action would dramatically improve service in ways that users actually value" (Lugg and Fischer 2009, 76). Although such an action would be extreme, especially for a research library, Slote's statement suggests that an initial rightsizing project should not cautiously nibble at a collection to remove a few obvious withdrawal candidates, but rather should take a proactive stand to withdraw tens of thousands of titles that have not been used recently, have a very low likelihood of ever being used again at that location, are widely held and easily obtainable elsewhere, and can disappear without affecting the overall collection integrity.

One of the major reasons why librarians now face the need to tackle huge rightsizing projects is that they have deferred for decades what should be routine periodic analysis and strategic withdrawals as an ongoing part of collection management. Instead, they built library extensions and storage facilities to house material that saw little use and was widely duplicated elsewhere. Many of these facilities are now at or near capacity. What is next in an era where claiming yet more storage space is a luxury few libraries can afford? This book discusses the reasons why libraries find themselves at this crossroads (or precipice, depending on the current situation in one's own library), reviews ways to rightsize the local physical collection (books, journals, microform, and more), and covers the various ways that libraries can participate in collaborative print retention projects.

Librarians well understand that some of today's outdated material will form tomorrow's foundation for historical scholarship. The problem, of course, lies in predicting which specific titles will form that foundation. The point is that not every library need maintain all the material, or even a significant portion of it, against the day when someone might need it. The vast majority of titles are widely duplicated; as long as librarians act responsibly to ensure that enough print copies exist across a region for future resource sharing, they can withdraw their own library's unused copies with clear consciences.

One backhanded benefit of the profession's having deferred rightsizing activities for decades is that current technology now allows the examination of many more variables to help identify withdrawal candidates. No longer must each individual library weed in a vacuum or must staff physically touch every single piece during the decision-making process. Today librarians can easily compare local holdings across their consortium, region, country, and throughout the world to make data-driven batch withdrawal decisions based not just on local circulation figures, but also on factors such as the relative scarcity of some titles, the holdings of specific peer or partner libraries, full-text availability from a stable vendor, and many other factors. In fact, some groups of libraries now undertake joint book rightsizing projects, the better to ensure retention of an adequate number of working copies within the membership. The majority of deselection decisions can be made based on the results of carefully crafted withdrawal candidate lists, rather than from volume-by-volume inspection in the stacks.

This book advocates establishing an overarching vision for rightsizing a library's physical collection and helps librarians develop a systematic, rules-based approach for evaluating these collections and making decisions about what to retain and what to deselect. However, the book will also assist librarians faced with sudden and externally imposed deadlines for reducing their collection's physical footprint. Although the focus is on evaluating and acting on the entire collection, or at least large portions of it, librarians may find the suggested methods helpful even if they only want to work with a small subset of the collection.

This book also offers practical advice on possible approaches to these tasks. It will explore ways to minimize the need for title-by-title reviews by embracing batch processing methods whenever possible. Some tasks are relatively easy to manage in-house; others require cooperation with peers, and some might best be undertaken in partnership with a consultant. This book emphasizes the benefits of creating an overall plan for proactive physical collection downsizing; building internal consensus; encouraging buy-in from constituents like university administrators and teaching faculty; project management; options for disposal of deselected material; and collaborating with other institutions. It reminds the reader that although a large, initial rightsizing project meets today's pressing needs, rightsizing is also a routine process that should take place at regular intervals.

In addition, rightsizing is not just a process that a single library undertakes in a vacuum. "Care is needed and support must be provided to ensure that libraries . . . do not make mistakes and withdraw materials that should be retained" for the greater good of the scholarly community at large (Demas and

Lougee 2011, 1). Many of the libraries tackling local rightsizing projects now will later participate in upcoming large-scale print management projects coordinated by the consortia to which they belong, and thus must take care to keep scarce works and stand ready to contribute to bigger projects in the future.

This book tries to separate discussions of books and journals. They are very different types of material; rightsizing decisions about them involve different factors and considerations. In addition, many libraries handle these separately rather than simultaneously when they rightsize. However, this separation is not always possible. Therefore, the discussion about collaborative print options covers joint storage facilities and distributed retention plans; because both books and journals may be included in either of these two options, both are discussed together.

The author acknowledges that generalizations can be misleading or dangerous. Academic libraries come in many types and sizes; a situation or best practice at a small private liberal arts college library may not even apply in a medical library at a research university. But there are also many similarities, and the challenge of not having enough space to house the physical collection, either because the library's size is decreasing, the collection is increasing, or both, is a problem for many academic libraries today. Readers can easily adapt many of the suggested actions to meet their own local needs.

The author hastens to clarify that a book focusing on decreasing the size of physical collections in academic libraries should not be misconstrued as a campaign against print. Print just happens to be the format in which libraries, both collectively and individually, hold an enormous amount of obsolete, highly duplicated, and low-use material. She advocates taking logical, strategic, and efficient steps to "de-select from collections . . . with the same dedication with which we selected for them" (Lugg and Fischer 2008b, 88). Rightsizing activities are not just about deselection, however; they include identifying what print material to keep: titles enjoying good use, titles of local interest, recently acquired items, and scarce titles that should be retained for the good of the scholarly community at large (even if they no longer interest anyone at the holding institution).

When faced with planning and implementing such a large project, sometimes under less than ideal circumstances, it is easy to focus on the mechanics of moving vast quantities of material out the door while perhaps losing sight of the reason for doing so. The author tried to keep at the forefront of the discussion the ultimate reason for rightsizing—shaping and presenting collections in the best possible way to improve the user experience. She agrees with the librarian who wrote that the "challenge for academic librarians is how to reduce the size of onsite collections without either destroying the soul of their libraries or sending their faculty to the barricades" (Barclay 2010, 54).

Rightsizing does not automatically imply crisis management, although libraries that have not undertaken substantial weeding projects within recent memory may well find themselves in crisis situations. It is also not a one-time fix. Rightsizing is an ongoing process that maintains a collection's optimal physical size by balancing such factors as:

- building current collections with a high potential for use in the short and medium term
- choosing electronic resources over print ones for many new acquisitions
- identifying local collections of distinction
- removing low-use titles that are widely held elsewhere
- participating in collaborative projects to reduce the number of consortial or regional lesser-used titles while retaining enough working copies to meet occasional demand
- withdrawing print and microform titles that now duplicate user-preferred, stable electronic access to the same material

Some redundancy has been built into this book, based on the expectation that some readers may focus only on sections relevant to their immediate needs. For example, in several places the book mentions the importance of determining if the library has *perpetual* access (not just access) to electronic content before identifying print titles as withdrawal candidates. However, this redundancy is not extensive and should not distract readers who work their way through the book from the beginning.

With few exceptions, the author decided not to name specific services or products. One reason is to avoid the appearance of endorsing one service or product over another; another is that these entities frequently change in scope, price, purpose, name, and corporate affiliation.

The interrelated topics of weeding, print retention, use studies, storage facilities, and collaborative collection management ventures all have long histories and extensive literatures. The author reviewed many articles on all these topics, but was selective in choosing which ones to cite. Many works detailed outdated processes or provided overviews of projects that ended decades ago or covered similar ground (e.g., many articles on "how we selected material to send to storage"). The author also skipped many articles focusing on narrow or specialized topics, such as weeding reference collections. This book does not take an exhaustive look into the past, but quotes from selected articles to give readers a glimpse of how academic librarians approached the continuous challenge of crowded shelves over the past hundred years. Understanding the roots and context of this challenge helps us appreciate how the problem of large no- and low-use academic collections developed over time, and how we can apply modern solutions to shape collections that our users need today and tomorrow.

"We need to learn that some books are dead books," wrote one scholar in 1949 (Colwell 1949, 195). This book will help today's librarians acknowledge this fact and determine the best way of identifying and handling the dead books in their own collections, while simultaneously retaining the ones with life in them yet—all with the purpose of improving their users' interactions with both the library in general and the collection in particular, both now and in the future.

1

Background

CHALLENGES FACING COLLEGES AND UNIVERSITIES

Before discussing the current state of academic libraries and their collections, it is useful to understand the larger environment of the current and changing states of their parent institutions.

Academe is undergoing transformational change. The number of simultaneously occurring influences, expectations, requirements, and opportunities is staggering. Some factors are new; others have increased in importance. They include, in no particular order:

- accountability to students, parents, donors, funding agencies, and taxpayers
- collaborations with international counterparts
- collaborations with business
- distance learning
- instructional redesign
- attracting and retaining high-caliber students
- employers' expectations that graduates demonstrate certain skills

- students' need to balance study, work, and leisure
- tuition costs and financial aid
- practical work experience or internships
- commitment to student success, including reasonable time to graduation
- special assistance for student groups (e.g., first-generation college attendees)
- international students
- increased emphasis on interdisciplinary scholarship
- faculty research and scholarship
- data management
- alumni relations
- campus computing
- state-of-the-art classrooms and laboratories
- compliance with state and federal laws
- diversity and multiculturalism
- international campuses
- attracting and retaining high-performing faculty
- post-graduation support
- placement services

Although many changes occur as reactions to external forces, forward-thinking administrators also embrace change to take proactive control over their institutions' futures. Many colleges and universities must compete aggressively to attract and retain the best students, and must demonstrate their ongoing commitment to quality education with more than a glossy brochure or flashy website. Prospective students and their parents now shop for what they perceive to be the best value, and assess everything from the professor-student ratio to the recreational center's facilities.

Partly as a result of all these changes, academic institutions value assessment more than ever. Assessment has always been a part of academic life, from various kinds of rankings to periodic visits from accreditation organizations, but today colleges and universities have become more proactive about assessment. Assessment offices have sprung up everywhere, and existing ones now enjoy greater visibility and significance. Their staff are devoted to measuring outcomes, developing workshops, assessing resources, conducting surveys, reporting program strengths and weaknesses and, most of all, suggesting and overseeing the implementation of changes to strengthen the institution.

ACADEMIC LIBRARIES TODAY

How do the changing environment and priorities of their parent institutions affect academic libraries? An important element is the expectation that all academic units have their own strategic plans that align with those of the central administration, and that those plans include assessment criteria. Libraries need to prove not only that their services benefit the institution's students and faculty, but also that these services are an integral part of student and faculty success. For decades, librarians' experiences with assessment merely involved reporting statistics, such as the number of classroom visits, the number of circulated items, the number of reference questions, and, of course, the number of volumes. Today universities require departments and programs to produce qualitative measures of effectiveness, not just quantitative ones.

Academic librarians have long grappled with the concepts of collection size, quality versus quantity, and maintaining a core collection. For many librarians, the number of volumes somehow conveyed the concept of value or prestige; having more volumes than the college library in the next city meant one's own institution was somehow superior. Not everyone subscribed to this concept, however. At a 1949 symposium called The Optimum Size of Libraries, Gosnell pointed out that "size is better defined in terms of the objectives of the library and the demands on it," and boiled the issue down to one sentence: "You keep the ones [books] they use, buy more, and throw out what is not used" (Gosnell 1950, 137). Trueswell explored this theme further when he wrote in 1976 that "in the no-growth collection new books must still be added, but little-used books will be removed at a comparable rate" (Trueswell 1976, 102). Engeldinger suggested that "if college librarians were to see decay in the stacks as a useful ally and use it as a preliminary guide to weeding collections, overall quality would be improved quickly" (Engeldinger 1999, 50).

Colwell described as an element of "institutional competition, institutional pride, and institutional jealousy" the desire to make one's own college better than others in the state or region (Colwell 1949, 197). The size of library collections has been a time-honored measurement of an institution's worth and value, encouraged by all kinds of comparative rankings and endorsed by library professional organizations. Size, of course, may have very little to do with value or quality (Engeldinger 1999, 50). Some would even argue that size actually diminishes a collection's value; Gosnell wrote about obsolete books obscuring the good books (Gosnell 1950, 138). Stueart warned against "a library's drive for quantity at the expense of quality" (Stueart 1985, 49). Itner stated that

> if collection development librarians were evaluated on the basis of how well the collections they built are used, they might take a livelier interest in weeding unused items. . . . Perhaps our professional problem is that we measure collection development success by how large the collections grow, rather than by how much service they provide in proportion to their size. (Itner 2006, 16)

"It is the use of the books not their numbers that gives evidence of meeting the needs of our stakeholders," Marcum pointed out in an article that equated unused books to a business's "idle inventory" (Marcum 2008, 15). A 1989 editorial titled "Ridding Collections of Deadwood" closed with this sentence: "Maybe we should begin to rank libraries according to the number of volumes *withdrawn* along with the number of volumes *added*" (Ridding Collections 1989, 3).

With more limited space options, college librarians are already accustomed to the idea of maintaining a collection at a certain fixed size. Librarians in larger libraries, particularly at research institutions, often have a tough time embracing this philosophy. They have worked, sometimes for decades, in an environment that cherished the notion of building collections not only for current use but also for future scholarship. They embraced, or at least concurred with, "the notion that an academic library must be large in order to be good" (Trueswell 1976, 73). The literature reflects a few other opinions, however. In 1947, for instance, Hardin pointed out that "either we must continually diminish the rate of increase or we must introduce what one might call a mortality factor" (Hardin 1947, 121). Several other authors wrote about the rate of obsolescence in library material in various disciplines. In 1976, Gore wrote, "The Alexandrian model persists through the unexamined faith that to be good a library *must* be vast and always growing. . . . [This faith] rests on nothing more solid than mistaken intuition, and [we should] consign it to the limbo of outworn dogmas" (Gore 1976, 3).

However, increased collection size does not necessarily translate into increased percentages of collection use. Academic libraries of all sizes contain large percentages of unused material. The very largest research institutions acquire titles to build as complete a collection as possible in many subject areas, knowing that some might not be used frequently. In general, however, librarians build collections to meet their users' anticipated needs. McCarthy described "demand . . . as a two-pronged thing, i.e. perceived long term demand and actual immediate needs" (McCarthy 2007, 350). Material acquired on a just-in-case basis to meet long-term demand may never be used, may be used a few times when relatively new, may be heavily used early in its shelf life, or may enjoy steady use over time. The problem is that it is nearly impossible to predict in advance into which of these categories a particular title will fall. In addition, some items that fill current needs, such as test preparation manuals and annual directories, may by definition have very short active shelf lives. Over time, the accumulation of thousands of items each year results in book stacks filled with low- and no-use titles interspersed with those relatively few titles that patrons actually use.

How do collections fulfill the library's mission? In the past, a library's mission included collecting material that supported the parent institution's curricular and research needs, and offering services, such as reference and instruction, that promoted the use of that collection to fill users' information needs. If rewritten today, in all but the largest research libraries, the mission statement might be changed to *providing access to* material that supports the parent institution's curricular and research needs. Today the total collection need not reside on campus; for most libraries the collections to which their users have access exist in many places besides on the local shelves. A growing part of it now exists digitally (and in the case of e-book patron-driven acquisitions plans, remains unpurchased until the moment of use), in off-site storage facilities, in consortial or regional cooperative storage facilities, or geographically close enough to allow resource sharing within a reasonable amount of time. This increased range of access means that the library can withdraw older or less-used material to which it can provide fast access on those relatively few occasions when it is needed, thus focusing its resources on building and maintaining a smaller local core of more frequently consulted material. Librarians may well decide to keep and maintain a small portion of the legacy print collection, but they can select items supporting a few specialized collections of distinction that define their own institutions, rather than struggle to maintain a comprehensive historical record in many subjects, especially when the material that comprises that historical record largely duplicates titles held in similar institutions across a state, region, or country. This means that librarians can develop plans to reduce their physical collections.

A ROSE BY ANY OTHER NAME

Librarians tap-dance around the words to use for the process of identifying and removing material that is no longer needed. The most common word is *weed*. Sometimes weeding is used to mean identifying material to send to a storage facility; at other times it means removing material permanently. The word has a negative connotation from its use in gardening and agriculture, where it indicates an unwanted, or even downright harmful, plant. The gardening analogy is useful because we understand that it is hard to see or appreciate the useful items (lovely blooms) if the shelves (flower beds) are choked with undesirable ones (weeds). Of course, some weeds are charming to look at, even though they choke out desirable or useful plants. But the negative connotation persists; Segal wrote that "weeding implies ridding an area of the undesirable, even infectious" (Segal 1986, 25). *Pruning* suggests a similar concept: thinning part of a plant and removing the deadwood so that the bush or tree may thrive.

Librarians have tried many other terms to avoid the the word *weed* and its negative connotation. A century ago, an anonymous no-nonsense librarian entitled his or her article "Discarding Useless Material" (1911). Some librarians have tried *retirement* (Ash 1963; Stueart 1985). A British author wrote about *obsolete stock* (Seymour 1972a).

An Australian used the term *stock stabilization* (Taylor 1976, 28). *Withdraw* is a popular choice. *Stack thinning* has been used (Trueswell, 1965). Williams called it *stock relegation* (Williams 1988). *Shelf-load reduction* has been used (Metz and Gray, 2005). Tongue in cheek, Manley suggested *library collection refreshment program* (Manley 2014, 80).

Deselection sounds very professional because it implies the thoughtful application of criteria to choose which items will leave the collection (Cooper and Norris, 2007; Thomas and Shouse, 2012; Ward and Aagard, 2008). A current favorite term is *print retention*, which shifts the emphasis away from the material leaving the shelves and focuses on the items chosen to remain. *Print archiving* is a relatively new term to describe a group of libraries' efforts to identify a certain low number of copies of works that will be retained in light storage (circulating) or dark storage (noncirculating preservation copies) on behalf of a group so that other members can then discard their own low-use copies if desired; this process often refers to runs of journal titles for which publishers have issued electronic backfiles (Bird and Ashoughian, 2012).

These terms provide librarians with polite words for a process that makes us wince: to be blunt, we are throwing away or otherwise disposing of unwanted material, but we want to convey that we give this activity the same careful attention that we do other aspects of our professional activities.

Although the term *weeding* no longer adequately describes the activity of making retention decisions about the physical collection, let's review some of the past discussion on this topic.

In 1976, Trueswell described weeding as a process whereby librarians make retention decisions by examining books and considering other factors such as circulation, age, subject area, and so on. He suggested that the results would be of "questionable value," but that "weeding decisions made by faculty experts are usually even less reliable. . . . Subject expertise counts for very little when the central problem is to predict mass behavior of a very large population of library users" (Trueswell 1976, 79–80).

In 1979, Bulick and his colleagues identified two main types of weeding: scientific and nonscientific. The nonscientific method requires experts to decide which items may have sufficient future value to justify keeping them; these decisions are subjective. The scientific approach involves developing models based on "tangible evidence" such as publication dates or circulation history, and then automating the retention decisions based on the model; these decisions are objective (Bulick, Sabor, and Flynn 1999, 48). Stueart emphasized the importance of "decisions [that] are based on facts and not simply on fancies or hunches" (Stueart 1985, 48). Similarly, Manley advised librarians not to employ "a random approach [and to] be systematic to avoid being accused of being arbitrary" (Manley 2014, 80).

Stueart considered the process to be linear:

> On the one hand, one must evaluate materials before purchasing them, and, on the other hand, one must re-evaluate their usefulness to the collection and then remove them, if they have lost their value. This removal

requires judgment just as selection does, and involves added pressures
that the initial purchase did not. (Stueart 1985, 49)

Unlike many of his contemporaries, Gosnell suggested that "weeding must be posited on accessibility to a central source that does keep the material that everybody else weeds" (Gosnell 1950, 138). In 1950, it was difficult to determine that another library would maintain the specific titles that one's own library weeded. It is much easier today.

Today most librarians would also agree that the objective method offers the best approach to rightsizing collections that may not have been seriously evaluated for decades and which contain a million or more pieces. It simply is not feasible to make item-by-item decisions, especially because while doing so, one must also spend time reviewing thousands of items that obviously should be retained. Now it is possible to build sophisticated withdrawal candidate models that not only weigh many more variables (Bulick's "tangible evidence") than was possible even a few years ago, but also automatically exclude titles that the library should keep (Bulick, Sabor, and Flynn 1979, 48).

Despite having more sophisticated tools for analysis today, the criteria to consider are still the same as they have been in the past. Two criteria that are almost always considered for books are the circulation history and the publication date. Since most academic libraries have used automated circulation systems for at least several decades, compiling circulation data is usually possible. It is important to know how many years of data are available (it will usually date from the installation of the system). Are there any reasons to doubt the accuracy of the data and, if so, what adjustments should be made to compensate? Does the system capture browsing or in-house activity for the same time period and, if so, will the data compilation incorporate it? Some older studies examined the amount of time between circulations to make use calculations; although this activity was possible when researchers could examine date-due stamps on books' circulation slips, this factor is now impossible to calculate from automated circulation systems designed to purge details once users return books. Librarians can now query their circulation systems to learn the total number of circulations and browses within a particular date range for a particular book, and also the date of last circulation, but interim details are not available.

WHY RIGHTSIZE?

So why use the term *rightsizing* instead of one of the other words or phrases used in the past? It is not just a new-fangled term to replace *weeding*. Rightsizing implies that librarians have developed the correct approach for shaping their libraries into the optimal size to serve their current constituents, not only with the right mix of material, in terms of both content and format, but also with the right set of services to obtain needed information quickly and efficiently if it is not available on-site. Rightsizing is not the ruthless culling of a library collection, nor is it just the tentative and apologetic removal of "safe" material like old editions of textbooks and superseded reference works. Rightsizing is the strategic, thoughtful, balanced, and planned process whereby librarians shape the collection by taking into account factors such as disciplinary differences; the impact of electronic resources on study, teaching, and research; the local institution's program strengths; previous use based on circulation statistics; and the availability of backup regional print copies for resource sharing.

Why do libraries contemplate rightsizing their collections? The reasons are many, complex, and often interrelated.

Space is an obvious reason; any growing physical collection cannot continue to occupy the same finite space indefinitely. Coupled with this is the need to use library space differently or pressure to meet other campus priorities by finding space for new or expanding programs and services. Even the most ardent opponent of weeding will agree that some material has long outlived any usefulness it might once have had. Resistance arises from unwillingness, for reasons which will be explored later, to part with any of it. As long ago as 1976 we find articles with statements about how the "position of the university library as a book depository is more and more being challenged as the emphasis is moving toward the library as an active service facility" (Taylor 1976, 28). Libraries should be vibrant information centers, not just warehouses for every item that ever entered the collection.

Large libraries that in the past seldom discarded anything have found that over time their collections have grown enormously, and that the cost of maintaining low-use material has risen out of proportion to the utility of having it available on-site or nearby, especially when much of this material is now available in digital equivalents. Maintaining no- and low-use material also represents real opportunity costs: in what other ways might the library have spent those maintenance funds for better-used and more-appreciated programs, services, and material?

Obsolescence is another major reason. The information in some books eventually goes out of date, although at different rates for different disciplines. Farber worried that for "many students, the mere fact that their library has a particular title in its collection means that the book is a valid work of scholarship" if they have not yet learned to evaluate the sources that they use (Farber 1998, 1).

Some parts of a library collection are now in less desirable formats, such as microform, and other pieces are outdated, physically deteriorated, duplicated in newer and preferred formats, or unused because of program changes or other reasons due to lack of local academic interest. Users increasingly prefer (or will at least use) electronic resources, which provide 24/7 access when visiting the library ranges from inconvenient to impossible, as is the case of growing numbers of distance learners.

A further concern is that as collections grow and age, users will find it increasingly difficult to identify and locate relevant material on crowded shelves. "Removing low use materials should increase the user success rate, decrease user frustration in search time and effort, and facilitate stacks maintenance" (Stueart 1985, 53). One drawback of a physical collection is that an item physically present on the shelves is more likely to be "rarely borrowed rather than one which is regularly borrowed, and there is danger that the reader, and perhaps especially the undergraduate, will come to regard the collection as comprising largely dead material which will induce in him a lack of confidence in the library stock, eventually hindering his discovery of live material" (Taylor 1976, 28).

Some studies have shown that books located on the uppermost and lowermost shelves are used less frequently than books shelved at more easily accessible levels. Circulation staff must spend more time shifting books to try to make more room. Crowded stacks may be prone to shelving errors, thus requiring more staff hours for shelf reading.

At the heart of any rightsizing project stands the core value that it is being undertaken to improve the user experience. Trueswell expressed this concept in 1965 when he wrote that "the criteria for stack thinning should be designed to help the library satisfy the requirements of the users of the library" (Trueswell 1965, 22). Librarians sometimes overemphasize other positive results of rightsizing, which might include recovering shelf space, removing material in less popular formats like microform, or avoiding the cost of building or expanding a storage facility. Although these are important outcomes, the project should ideally be undertaken in the same user-centric spirit as collection development: as a complement to the activity of building the collection to meet user needs, rightsizing shapes the collection to help users find relevant material quickly and easily. Manley wrote that the "library that operates without an ongoing and systematic weeding strategy is not giving its users the professional attention they should expect" (Manley 2003, 80).

Thomas and Shouse identified two traditional reasons and two newer ones for weeding. Traditionally, libraries weeded to create space for new material and to create "a more usable, up-to-date, and attractive collection." They added two new reasons: "the changing perception of libraries from book warehouses to service points, and the . . . radical shift from print use to electronic use of scholarly content" (Thomas and Shouse 2012, 92).

Is rightsizing perfect? No; it is inevitable that there will be a few mistakes in a large retroactive rightsizing project that involves tens or hundreds

of thousands of volumes, or even in the ongoing routine collection maintenance that rightsizing also requires. None of these errors are irreparable if
librarians focus on withdrawing low-use books that are widely held in print
elsewhere or on journals that either have electronic equivalents or are readily
available through interlibrary loan (ILL). Developing and building consensus
for thoughtful and strategic withdrawal criteria reduce the likelihood of many
errors. It is important to focus on the overall benefits of reducing the physical
collection, rather than agonizing about the few items that may need to be
borrowed or replaced later. "It is probable that the greatest mistake is made by
the librarian who refuses to weed or by the user who considers it unnecessary"
(Martin and Manch 1971, 599).

THE DIGITAL REVOLUTION

The widespread availability of digital format for both new and retroactive content has revolutionized the scholarly world and the libraries that support it.
Libraries face many new challenges with this new format, including how to
acquire it; how to describe it; how to catalog it; how to provide access to it;
how to promote it to their users; how to teach best practices for using it; how
to produce it; how to convert print format into digital; and how to store and
maintain it. After centuries of handling tangible items, librarians now must
handle the intangible. It has not been an entirely smooth transition, and it is
not yet over. For some decades to come we will continue managing collections
in both formats. Despite several massive efforts, it is not "all on the Web" yet.
Although patrons have generally embraced the electronic journal article, some
still resist the electronic book in certain disciplines or for particular uses.
There are also significant legal and economic barriers that prevent the universal availability of all previously printed works in digital form.

Two of the major types of digital works that libraries acquire for their
users are journals and books (which also include reports, government documents, theses, dissertations, and similar items). New works may still be
issued in both print and digital formats, although not necessarily simultaneously. Sometimes the works may be digitized versions of those that originally appeared in print some time ago, such as journal backfiles or decades-old
books that were created as part of digitization projects. In yet other cases,
the digital versions may include features that were not included in the print
equivalent, such as links to external sites or to data files. (Other formats, such
as music and film, may be digitized, but these are beyond the scope for this
book.)

Even without the digital revolution, many libraries would face severe
space crises. In some respects, however, the advent and widespread acceptance

(or at least tolerance) of stable digital substitutes and digital-only scholarly objects have made it easier for librarians to accept the inevitability of rightsizing, especially when the digital duplicates the print, as is the case with many journals.

Libraries provide electronic access to the journal literature in several ways.

First, they may license a subject-specific aggregator database that includes some full-text articles. These articles are usually in PDF versions, but sometimes will be in HTML format and may not include features like photographs or tables that appeared in the original. The aggregator may decide, or the publisher stipulate, to limit access to selected articles from a journal title or to articles from a certain range of years. Coverage for particular journal titles may only be selective. Almost all journal titles employ a moratorium during which time recent articles may be indexed but are not available in full text; the moratorium periods can vary by title or by publisher from several months to several years. It is important to note that aggregator content is licensed, not purchased; the aggregator may remove articles without warning or notice and for a variety of reasons that include a publisher deciding to withdraw its full-text content from an aggregator's database. As a rule, librarians should not base print retention decisions on the availability of content licensed from aggregators; however, an exception will be highlighted in the discussion of JSTOR below.

The second major way in which libraries provide e-journal access for their users is by subscribing to individual titles or to packages of titles, either directly from the publishers or through third-party subscription agents. These subscriptions are not usually governed by a purchase agreement, but rather by a licensing agreement or contract. The license spells out what rights the library and its users have to the content. Examples might be that the library will not provide any part of the content to a for-profit organization, or that the library retains the right to provide articles through resource sharing within the boundaries of the copyright law. An electronic-resources librarian should review the licenses and negotiate them as needed, for example, to be sure that there is a resource sharing clause in all licenses. Subscriptions, by definition, start at a specified time and go forward as long as the library pays the renewal invoices. If librarians later drop a subscribed title, the library retains access rights to the volumes for which it has already paid (this should be spelled out in the license agreement).

The majority of academic libraries have stopped print subscriptions to most periodical titles and now rely on electronic access. Exceptions include some general or popular magazines and titles such as trade publications from small publishers that do not offer electronic versions of their titles. Some publishers offer electronic-only subscriptions; some offer print *or* electronic subscriptions; a few insist on providing print *and* electronic subscriptions, although in this last case many libraries simply discard the print issues and rely on the electronic access. Managing print subscriptions is far less onerous than in the past because libraries now handle so few print journal issues. Managing electronic subscriptions can become complicated, however, for reasons such as missing issues or the sudden inability to access a title, issue, article, or a publisher's entire site.

Third, a few aggregators have negotiated permanent and stable electronic access to long runs of journal titles from a variety of publishers. JSTOR is an example of this type of aggregator. It groups these titles into various packages that a library can purchase outright or pay for over a period of years. For active titles, moratoria varying from three to seven years preclude access to recent issues. Some titles stretch as far back as the nineteenth century. Some of these types of aggregators offer plans both for stable access to various publishers' backfiles as well as an optional subscription plan for recent issues of selected titles; a library subscribing to both plans provides users with seamless access to past and recent content. Librarians accept that because titles in these types of aggregators' lists are stable, print retention decisions can be made based on those parts of these aggregators' journal lists that the library holds. Librarians should be careful, however, to pay attention to moratoria dates and avoid withdrawing print volumes that correspond to years still in an aggregator's moratorium zone, which would result in removing all local access for those years unless the library also has a current subscription to those titles from another source.

Fourth, partial or complete backfiles are available from a variety of free or open access sources on the Web. These include:

- digitized issues of titles that fall into the public domain (pre-1923 in the United States)
- open access journals
- government-issued serial titles
- older content that publishers have digitized for free access

Libraries often harvest these types of journal titles and add bibliographic records to their catalogs or discovery layers to make it easier for users to find them. Exercise caution if using open web access to support decisions for withdrawing the corresponding print volumes. Judge the source of the econtent very carefully. Some producers of this type of econtent are very stable, others less so. The quality of the digitized images in free web content is also a significant concern for many titles.

Fifth, publishers offer libraries backfiles of their journal content. These can be acquired as single titles, as bundles of titles, or as a blanket acquisition of all titles from volume 1 to the point where subscriptions began, or, if the library does not subscribe to some titles, to several years back. Large backfile acquisitions from major publishers may be coordinated on the consortial level. Note that publishers often offer special deals or are more open to price negotiations towards the end of a fiscal year.

Academic libraries typically employ some or all of these techniques to provide electronic journal content for their users. One unavoidable byproduct of this approach is that some of the same content is available in multiple ways. For example, selected articles from a particular journal will be available in HTML through an aggregator's subject database; a complete run of the same title (minus the most recent five years) appears via an aggregator that negotiated with the publisher; and the last ten years through the present are also available because the library subscribes to the journal.

Libraries also acquire electronic books in a variety of ways. Some are selected on a title-by-title basis as part of traditional collection development activities. Some arrive as part of approval plans. Others are part of databases that include some full-text books or reports. Some are included in subscription e-book packages. Some are part of massive e-book packages purchased from single publishers or from a coalition of multiple publishers. Librarians may add open access books or full-text government reports to their collections, or may load records with links to full-text books from one or more of the major book digitization projects. Patron-driven acquisitions e-book plans offer the option of adding thousands of e-book titles that await patron use to trigger purchases. Library catalogs and discovery layers often include full-text reports, dissertations, and theses from the local institutional repository.

The growing availability of an increasing amount of electronic access to no- or low-use print items often provides the initial impetus for librarians to start thinking about undertaking a rightsizing project. Despite this rapid increase in electronic access to the retrospective literature, however, a lot of rightsizing activity takes place without a digital safety net.

PROJECT GENESIS

What causes the initial spark for considering and then implementing a rightsizing project? It can emerge from any one of a variety of internal and external sources.

Sometimes the first push comes from university administrators who have identified some portion of current library space that they prefer to use for another purpose. If that space contains part of the physical collection, then some combination of weeding, shifting, or relocating the material will be necessary. Even if the earmarked space does not contain library material, the library administrators may want to reorganize the remaining space in a way that involves reducing or removing part of the collection.

Another potential external influence is the library's membership in a consortium that is embarking on some kind of joint print retention plan. Simply participating in such a plan does not necessarily embrace the full concept of rightsizing at the local level, but involvement may be the impetus that encourages librarians to consider increasing the scope of their print retention activities to include the local collection.

Uninfluenced by any external triggers, library administrators may, for a variety of reasons, suggest or mandate a rightsizing project. The stacks and storage facilities may be full, with no reasonable expectation of obtaining new space to contain growing collections. A new facility may be a possibility, but the administrators may not want to move decades of unused or outdated material into the new space without some kind of evaluation. Newly constructed primary library space on a central campus may be configured very differently from traditional buildings, perhaps with an emphasis on shared learning spaces and on access to digital information. Space for physical collections may be limited mainly to a few years of recent works that cannot be obtained electronically. If constructing a new facility is not possible, administrators may want to reconfigure current library space drastically to meet changing learning and research needs.

The impetus for rightsizing can also come from below. Librarians responsible for managing collections, circulation, storage space, or branch libraries may reach the conclusion that it is no longer feasible or useful to maintain increasingly unused stacks crowded with journal volumes available in a more popular format or with large numbers of books that are seldom consulted. Individually or collectively, these librarians will broach the topic of weeding the collection. If they do not specifically advocate rightsizing the physical collection as defined in this book, their administrative supervisors should seriously consider upgrading a request to weed trouble spots to a more strategic and comprehensive rightsizing effort.

RESISTANCE TO RIGHTSIZING

Roy's exhaustive 1994 encyclopedia article on weeding traced arguments against weeding in the literature as far back as the 1890s (Roy 1994, 368–98). There will always be people who oppose permanently removing material— especially large amounts of it—from a library's collection, no matter how outdated, redundant, or otherwise unused it has become over time. In fact, some detractors "may have strong conceptual objections to the de-prioritization of print even if they themselves rarely or never make use of library print collections" (Housewright 2010, 38). Librarians who, at least initially, view this activity as being anything from a necessary evil to an unmitigated disaster will, not surprisingly, approach the process unwillingly. This book hopes to make the case that academic libraries have reached a point in their history where they can proactively develop reasoned—and reasonable—rightsizing plans that shape their physical collections so that their users can easily find and use the material that has been designated for retention, while also maintaining easy access to formerly held material through arrangements with other libraries. "The problems of collecting are difficult; the problems of uncollecting are difficulty squared," observed Hardin (Hardin 1947, 122). Librarians who themselves take the first steps towards developing deselection plans as carefully as they developed their selection programs will find the experience much more pleasant than one undertaken in haste as a result of externally applied pressures and deadlines.

Although Wezeman's article "Psychological Barriers to Weeding" was published in 1958, many of his observations hold true today. He commented that despite a professional history of cooperation, many librarians are "bibliographic isolationists" focused on the "small sample of books" in their own collections. He called it a "professional disgrace" and pointed out the "bad impression created by shelves cluttered with old, outdated, useless material." In his opinion, "the cheapest, most effective, but often least used piece of library equipment is the wastebasket" (Wezeman 1958, 638).

For the most part, print journals are now in an obsolete format, at least from the patron perspective. Librarians sometimes refer to the older parts of their collections as the "legacy collection" or even as the "legacy print collection." McCarthy pointed out that these terms are ambiguous (McCarthy 2007, 347). Does the legacy collection include everything that is not electronic? Everything in the storage facility? Everything that has not been checked out recently? Do we intend to assign some vague concept of value to this material? The word *legacy* does not necessarily imply value; an heir may be excited about the prospect of receiving a legacy until he discovers that Aunt Martha left him her extensive collection of videotapes.

Another reason some librarians regard rightsizing unfavorably is the nagging feeling that perhaps not all the unused titles are truly unwanted. Surely somebody could use them! We know that "material which is out of date for modern use may be valuable in historical studies" (Seymour 1972a, 138). No matter how apparently unneeded a book may seem today, it is a product of its time and culture, and we cannot guess what a future scholar might glean from it. Perhaps books on a certain topic will be of interest to a researcher thirty or three hundred years from now. Could someone in a developing country benefit from these outdated textbooks? The general truth is that if these books have not been used recently by the local user community *and* if there are also sufficient copies in the library community at large, then most libraries do not need to keep them.

Some librarians raise the issue of professional ethics when it comes to withdrawing parts of their collections. Rather than analyzing titles based on circulation history and availability elsewhere, should we instead consider our own feelings? Should weeding be considered good or bad, rather than simply one aspect of collection management? Bazirjian explored these questions and concluded that "we have inherited a negative connotation of what is a beneficial and necessary library function." Instead of feeling guilty, she asked, why not "look at discarding as an art, as a process which requires the same skill and competency as is needed in book selection or acquisition?" When discarding books, she recommends honesty, objectivity, and competency, the same qualities that librarians exercise when selecting material. A conservative approach or squirrelling tendencies are not in patrons' best interests (Bazirjian 1990, 138).

It is impossible to embark on a large rightsizing project without thinking of the millions of dollars spent over the previous decades to buy all the material being evaluated as potential withdrawal candidates. Yes, the money spent building the collection was considerable, and much of the material that librarians purchased had value to the users at the time. But now many of those items no longer retain much of that value. Books have life cycles (i.e., introduction, growth, maturity, and decline), just as other products and services do. Universities routinely divest themselves of old and obsolete items such as laboratory equipment, computers, groundskeepers' trucks, dormitory furniture, classroom desks, overhead projectors, cafeteria plates, office fixtures, the president's car, and many more. Difficult as it may be to accept, library material can eventually fall into the same category as outdated equipment.

Consciously or unconsciously, librarians struggle with this concept of value. An item's purchase price is one indication of value. It is difficult to discard a book that originally cost 300 dollars even if that book was never used, or saw moderate use early in its life but none in the most recent two decades. The fact that the title is now advertised on the used book market for 10 dollars (with few takers) may not diminish the concept of a higher value related to the initial cost. The book's content has some value, too. An author devoted time to writing it, and a publisher's willingness to produce, market, and distribute it also indicates value. Then there is the possibility that at some time in the unknowable future, someone will want to consult the item and will draw from it some insight that is impossible today. How does one assign a value to that possible future use? The point is that librarians also have a stake in the current value of the collection as a whole as it relates to current users. A slimmed-down yet vibrant collection, evaluated and winnowed periodically to maintain relevance, is a gift to busy patrons. So are robust and responsive services that obtain material quickly from other sources, be it a recent item that the library never obtained or an older one that the library never held (or might have previously held but which is no longer in the collection). The measure of a library's value lies largely with the users who are best served by a relevant collection coupled with services that rapidly acquire other material that they need.

Of course, librarians recognize that some copies of nearly every book should be retained and, in fact, preserved. We should be careful not to discard titles held by only a handful of other libraries, and we should make conscious efforts to maintain a few copies of even the most obscure or outdated material as part of consortial arrangements or for the general good of the scholarly community. The main point is that hundreds of academic libraries do not need to maintain hundreds or even dozens of copies of the same obsolete book.

Although librarians undertake weeding activities at least in part to make the collection more relevant for users, some patrons also have emotional reactions to it. Previous negative press about other libraries' weeding projects means that librarians often approach rightsizing projects with trepidation, because they fear adverse publicity or that they will be held personally responsible for exercising their professional judgment in pursuit of an administrative goal. Others approach the topic with a tongue-in-cheek attitude; Ramirez humorously suggested, for instance, that weeding tasks take place secretly at night, by flashlight, and by librarians dressed in black (Ramirez 2013, 10). Manley seconded this advice with the directive to "get rid of the goods in the middle of the night under cloak of darkness" (Manley 2014, 80).

Why does weeding generate feelings as varied as fear, guilt, panic, distaste, and rebellion? Sometimes librarians duck the issue by saying they are too busy to weed, although one hopes that these same people do not also declare that they are too busy to select books, answer reference questions, or serve as liaisons with academic departments.

Another stumbling block is the concept of the book as sacred object. In 1911, an anonymous author summed up the feeling perfectly: "When a book once gets on the shelves, it seems to acquire in the eyes of most librarians a peculiar virtue and reverence, irrespective of any service it may render" (*New York Libraries* 1911, 221). It is somehow difficult to view an unused library book in the same light as, say, an outdated computer with a floppy disk drive. Other concerns revolve around the time needed for old-fashioned title-by-title reviews; these include the fear of making mistakes, incurring faculty displeasure, discarding a title that someone might want one day, acute awareness of the high original cost of many of the withdrawal candidates, and the general acknowledgment that at any given moment in one's professional career, there are far more pressing (and interesting) things to do than discarding books.

The literature is full of articles about the need to identify material that should be removed from a collection. Some authors take a serious approach. Others try to defuse a potentially frightening topic with lighthearted titles, such as "Weeding without Tears" (Roy 1990), "Don't Judge a Book by Its Dust" (Kelley 2013), and even the author's own "The Dark Side of Collection

Management" (Ward and Aagard 2008). The last article chronicled the author's first foray into data-driven collection analysis that considered, among other things, consortial partner holdings and the number of copies in the research community at large. The title reflects her feelings at the time of cautiously beginning what she now calls rightsizing and handling a project (identifying short and scattered serial runs to withdraw from a storage facility) which, if assumptions turned out to be erroneous, would do the least damage to the collection. Today she cringes at that title. Rightsizing is a valid, necessary, respectable, and strategic part of collection management, but in many libraries it has been neglected for so long that the thought of tackling even a small piece of it raises fear and doubt. Moving in stages from doubt and uncertainty to embracing what is in essence the natural path of a collection's life cycle is a journey, and not everyone travels at the same speed.

STAKEHOLDERS

Who are the major stakeholders in a rightsizing project? They are the library administrators, selected university administrators, the project manager, library colleagues, library staff, teaching faculty, and students. Other stakeholders might include donors, taxpayers at a state-supported institution, and the scholarly community at large. Not everyone in these groups will be aware that they are stakeholders in the library's project, but it is the librarians' responsibility to identify stakeholders and to consider the project's potential impact on these groups, especially in terms of what Schonfeld called the "emotionally vexing element" (Schonfeld 2011, 142). One author identified

> at least three groups of invested parties: the traditionalists who want the paper library to always exist; the faux traditionalists who want electronic delivery, but also want a library to smell and look like the British Museum; and the brave new worlders who hold no sentiment for the edifice of the library and simply want information as fast as possible. (Scherlen 2004, 118)

Users from most stakeholder groups may fall into any of these categories, although in different percentages. For example, most students just want information quickly, but individual donors, teaching faculty, administrators, and even library employees may identify with any of the three groups.

Library Administrators

Library administrators should discuss the proposed rightsizing project with top university administrators such as the provost or vice president for academic affairs. That person should understand the necessity of the project, approve of it, and be prepared to support the library's decision if approached by others with less enthusiastic opinions. Of course, some rightsizing projects get under way as a direct result of administrators' plans for part of library space; in those cases the support will be especially strong.

Project Manager

The project manager is a major stakeholder. The library administrators should make this appointment thoughtfully both in terms of selecting the right person and allocating a sufficient portion of that person's time to managing the project. A project manager does not merely oversee a summer weeding project in a single location, but supervises a system-wide project to coordinate a strategic and significant reduction in the size of the library's physical collection. In the early stages, the project manager will be instrumental in working with staff and local colleagues to explain the necessity for and benefits of a print reduction plan. The work may very well entail a multiyear commitment. It may also involve collaborating with colleagues at other institutions, a consortial coordinating office, or a consultant. A library's rightsizing project manager may become a key player in a consortial plan as a member of a steering committee, or even as the major consortial representative, to explore options, interview consultants, build group consensus on project parameters, negotiate with organizations that will collect the deselected material, and more. Speaking or writing opportunities sometimes emerge. A successful early implementer may later serve as an unofficial mentor to colleagues in other institutions who are just beginning a similar undertaking. The project manager should be both goal- and detail-oriented, and have the ability to plan, implement, oversee, and assess staff and processes. The ability to build consensus and be a problem solver is also an asset. Because a rightsizing project potentially represents a major career opportunity, the manager has a significant professional interest in its success beyond any local accomplishments.

Library Colleagues

Library colleagues form another important stakeholder group. As discussed earlier, librarians' initial reactions to the notion of weeding range from support, to reluctance, to apprehension, to adamant opposition. Segal wrote of librarians' feelings of "regret and anxiety" about weeding and their perception that the process of deselection is an "unpleasant duty" (Segal 1986, 25–26). Many colleagues will need to hear the reasons for and review the rightsizing process several times before beginning to understand and eventually embrace (or at least accept) the rationale behind it. The project organizers and manager should offer several different venues for presenting the project and for answering questions. These may comprise an agenda item at a collection development meeting, an informal brown bag discussion, attendance at a session with the rightsizing consultant, and, when indicated, individual meetings with colleagues. The library administrators, in concert with the project manager, should demonstrate their firm support of and belief in the project.

Library Staff

Remember to keep library staff in the loop. The support staff who will be removing items from the shelves, moving hundreds of boxes or bins around campus, or deleting thousands of records from the catalog should have a good understanding of why this is happening. Informing the staff can take place at unit or department meetings, between supervisors and key staff, between the project manager and key staff, and in the library newsletter, as well as at all-staff meetings.

Teaching Faculty

Working with the teaching faculty sometimes raises the thorniest issues. In academic libraries, the faculty's involvement to collection building ranges from making almost all of the selection decisions to submitting occasional book purchase requests. A comment from 1949 applies equally now: "In most institutions today the professor considers the development of the library solely in terms of his individual needs. Neither he nor his colleagues plan the future of the library in terms of the institution's need" (Colwell 1949, 196). Decades of professorial book selection result in many library books that were of interest to one person who is now affiliated with another institution, currently pursuing other research topics, or retired.

Although it is a sound idea for the library's dean or director to present the reasons and methodology for the work to the library's faculty advisory group, how (or should) the general faculty be informed or involved? Faculty may exhibit a similar range of opinions as library colleagues, everything from complete indifference through militant outrage. The reasons for the range of faculty reactions are a complex mixture based on factors such as academic discipline, how much a faculty member uses library resources and whether these are chiefly the journal literature or the book literature, degree of involvement in the library facility (main building or branch) housing the material in his or her subject area, degree of involvement in collection development, comfort level with electronic resources, and experience with an efficient and effective interlibrary loan service. Faculty members may focus on the fact that something is being taken away from them, notwithstanding the fact this material is outdated, unused, readily and quickly available from partner libraries through interlibrary loan, and, in many cases, already replaced by electronic access to the identical content. What if someone wants it someday? What about scholars who prefer print books to electronic books? How about the argument that the ability to browse the shelves for serendipitous discovery will be diminished? How will our university stack up against the rival downstate or in national rankings if our library volume counts drop dramatically? How will accreditation organizations react? And finally, "I understand that we need to reduce the collection for space reasons, but I want final review authority for every item in my subject area."

In 1954, in preparation for a project to transfer books to a storage facility, one librarian described meeting with members of the faculty in the department he served, then talking with the department chair to come to an agreement on selection criteria, and finally allowing the "opportunity to examine all books selected for transfer, with the prerogative of returning to the shelves any that they decided it would be undesirable to remove" (Walsh 1954, 378). Librarians undertaking a weeding project in the 1980s

> expected a negative reaction to the project on the part of some faculty
> members. . . . Each [academic] unit was asked to appoint a weeding
> liaison. . . . Librarians never argued with the faculty over individual titles.
> We felt that this would be a fruitless endeavor and, given the purpose of
> the faculty review, counterproductive. (Harloe 1984, 265)

When the librarian who weeded the political science section at one library invited faculty to review her choices, they sent a third of the titles back to the shelves. She sampled 10 percent of the returned books two years later and found that less than 7 percent of them had been checked out since their return (Banks 2002, 115). Another librarian witnessed the opposite: "due to their subject expertise, faculty tended to pull more books that the librarians" (Dubicki 2008, 134).

With large, time-sensitive rightsizing projects there may simply not be time for faculty review and input. Librarians should build understanding and trust with their constituents regarding the deselection criteria and the librarians' expertise and ability to make good withdrawal decisions.

Some faculty resist the idea of removing titles to remote storage (never mind sending them to a regional collaborative storage facility or actually withdrawing some of them) on the grounds that "great scholarly moments" occur serendipitously while browsing the library stacks. Barclay's article "The Myth of Browsing" agrees that these moments can happen, but that there are many reasons why this argument is fallacious, including the fact that users' direct interactions with academic library stacks are only a few decades old and that centuries of scholarship occurred during the closed stack era; high-demand books are likely to be in circulation and many others are missing or otherwise unaccounted for; books covering multidisciplinary subjects can only be physically shelved in a single place; and books on high or low shelves may be missed. Barclay believed that online search tools uncover far more relevant scholarly material—in one's own library, in local storage facilities, in consortial repositories, or in places otherwise accessible through interlibrary loan services—than can possibly be discovered by a stroll through the local stacks. Barclay concluded:

> While the presence of books . . . send[s] the message that one has entered a place of scholarship and thoughtfulness . . . there is no evidence to suggest that the presence of two million mostly unused books sends such a message any better than the presence of 200,000 heavily used books. (Barclay 2010, 54)

Librarians try to accommodate these concerns in many ways. Clearly explaining the rationale for the rightsizing project is helpful. Asking subject liaisons to communicate with their departments is one approach; the faculty have working relationships with the liaisons and trust their judgment in matters of library policy and practice. Many liaisons have advanced degrees in the same subject areas as the teaching faculty and can emphasize that their educational background gives them the ability to shape withdrawal criteria to ensure that no heavily used or vital titles will be removed. Anticipating possible questions to prepare answers in advance, in consultation with the project manager and library administration, is a smart move. Having a specific need or goal, such as needing to reassign or repurpose library space, may actually be helpful when explaining the project, but when libraries undertake rightsizing projects without an obvious impetus for doing so, it may be harder for faculty to understand the rationale. Referring to the results of Ithaka S+R's triennial faculty surveys (available at www.sr.ithaka.org/research-publications) may be helpful to show that over time, faculty in many disciplines at many universities have become increasingly comfortable with using electronic journals, and with the idea of withdrawing the print equivalent and relying on the digital counterparts (Housewright, Schonfeld, and Wulfson 2013).

Students

Although the institution's students form a stakeholder group because they are usually the major users of the library's collection, it is generally not necessary to involve them directly in any phase of the rightsizing project unless they are included in a general publicity plan to alert the campus of an upcoming project.

Donors

Donors form another possible stakeholder group. Today many libraries no longer routinely accept any and all book donations. They have clear and posted guidelines stipulating that librarians will make the final decisions about whether to accept a gift, how it will be classified, where it will be housed, and what will be its final disposition. Special arrangements may be made when accepting extraordinary donations (such as the personal papers of famous alumni), but for the vast majority of gifts, the donor should have no expectation either that the library will accept anything and everything offered to it or that the library will keep any accepted material in perpetuity.

Taxpayers

For institutions that receive at least some funding from their states, taxpayers form another possible stakeholder group. The notion of "the book as sacred object" may emerge again. People who would never object to the chemistry department discarding damaged and outdated laboratory equipment become alarmed at the notion of a library discarding outdated or unused books. People regard books as having intrinsic value, even when they are old, worn, outdated, or unused. Posting a deselection policy that is an upfront statement about the necessity and goals of the rightsizing project and highlighting the approval of the university administration go a long way towards defusing these anxieties.

Authors

What about the authors whose books are being withdrawn? Manley recounted being presented with a library discard of one of his books for an autograph. Initially taken aback, he later realized that the book was "out of date, irrelevant to the times, and bordering on tedious. . . . It did not represent my best work." He expressed relief that the book was "out of circulation" (Manley 2014, 80).

The Scholarly Community

The scholarly community at large is a stakeholder in any library's rightsizing project. Scholars have a right to expect that the professionals who manage libraries will take reasonable care, at both the individual and collective levels, to ensure that scarce material will be preserved and maintained in sufficient quantities to be available now and for future generations. This does not mean, however, that scholars can expect that their own institution will necessarily maintain locally every low-use title that they might ever need.

Consortial Partners

Consortial partners form another stakeholder group. It is likely that in the future many library consortia will undertake cooperative print management projects on a much larger scale than single-library efforts. If many members have previously conducted large weeding projects without giving much thought to the possible impact outside of their local environment, it is possible that the larger effort may introduce some unexpected inequities between members that have already reduced their collections and those that have not. Of course, there are many reasons why a single library cannot wait for consortial action, but at the very least local retention decisions should be based, in part, on how many other copies exist within the consortium. When rightsizing, a single library should keep scarce and rare titles even if local patrons no longer use them. Not only will these titles be maintained for the scholarly community in general, but they will also form at least part of the library's contribution to future consortial cooperative print management efforts. A library cannot expect to borrow scarce titles from other institutions if it does not make a good effort to maintain its own scarce copies to lend when needed.

How should librarians communicate with stakeholders about a rightsizing project? Discussing the importance of a major rightsizing project with selected campus administrators has already been mentioned. Some librarians feel that rightsizing activities, as a routine aspect of collection management, should not require any special explanation to the user population any more than would plans to shift the collection or conduct an inventory. They feel comfortable posting the library's deselection policy on the library web page, answering questions if asked, and leaving it at that. Other librarians take a proactive approach and develop communication plans that involve actions such as displays or posters in the library, articles in library newsletters and other campus publications, special web pages, and announcements at departmental faculty meetings. At one college, librarians sent a letter to the faculty "describing the reasons for the weeding project along with a list of frequently asked questions" (Soma and Sjoberg 2011, 22). At another institution, librarians published an article in the campus faculty/staff newsletter that

> presented an overview of the shelf-load problem, outlined the strategies that would be employed, and invited academic departments to participate in the process. . . . Perhaps the primary benefit of the article in the long run was that the University Libraries could indicate to critics who surfaced in subsequent years that we had described our plans and invited comment. We were also able to demonstrate that our guidelines focused on a careful stewardship of the collection and that every effort would be made not to discard items of historical interest or held by only a few libraries. (Metz and Gray 2005, 274)

Besides communicating with stakeholders *en masse*, the library administrators should determine the path for any formal individual questions or complaints. Liaison librarians can field informal questions, but one person— perhaps the project manager—should be designated to respond promptly to other questions. Many of the questions will be similar, so standard replies can be developed for many of them. Librarians at one university found it helpful to provide examples of the materials being withdrawn so that people could better understand that removing old textbooks and other outdated material would not harm the collection (Metz and Gray 2005, 275).

What role should stakeholders play in a rightsizing project? As with the question of communication above, the answer varies depending on the institution, the librarians' philosophy, and the plan. Some libraries involve the faculty in the decision-making process, whereas others view the work as part of librarians' normal professional responsibilities. The literature discusses many instances in which faculty have reviewed lists or carts of books, or have even come in to the library to review shelves of books in their areas of expertise. Results varied, just as they do when librarians perform the same tasks. Some faculty did a good and objective job; others began their work enthusiastically, but later lost interest or could no longer find the time to complete their assignments; and others preferred not to be involved at all. Some librarians involved other patrons in the process, such as by placing bookmarks in withdrawal candidates on the shelf several months in advance and inviting patrons to write comments if they felt that the items should be retained (Tobia 2002, 96). There are pros and cons of involving others in the deselection or review process. Subject experts suggest retaining some useful titles, but on the other hand, they may, consciously or not, introduce subjective elements into a deselection process that started out as an objective one employing use data or stable electronic access as major deselection criteria.

In the project-planning stages, librarians should certainly discuss the issues of communication and faculty involvement and make clear decisions about both from the outset.

USE STUDIES

Academic librarians know that their patrons seldom or never use many of the books in their collections. Comprehensive use studies based on circulation data that explore this phenomenon date back at least as far as 1950s.

In 1950, Webb reported that 90,000 volumes from a total of 135,000 in his college library had not circulated in the past year. He also conducted a study of five years of circulation activity for books in selected call number ranges and concluded that 60 percent of the books in his library were "excess baggage." He determined that 66,000 books could be discarded without damaging the collection (Webb 1950, 146).

An active researcher on this topic, Trueswell conducted one famous study in which he concluded that 20 percent of the collection accounted for 80 percent of the total use (Trueswell 1969). This finding has become known as the

"80/20 rule." In another study he found that in two libraries at one research university, 40 percent and 25 percent, respectively, of their current collections would meet 99 percent of patrons' needs. He suggested that 60 to 75 percent of those collections could be removed without inconveniencing users (Trueswell 1965). In his 1976 study, Trueswell used the last circulation date to illustrate a method by which a library could determine what percentage of its collection could be safety weeded since the remainder would form a core collection that would meet almost all user demand (Trueswell 1976). Many of the graphs in this article (as well as in Trueswell's earlier 1965 article) look eerily similar to graphs that modern librarians may recognize from Chris Anderson's 2006 book *The Long Tail: Why the Future of Business Is Selling Less of More*. Anderson found that retailers and e-retailers make most of their money selling many units of a few products, although there is also profit in selling a few units each of many items (the long tail). Likewise, Trueswell showed that relatively few of a library's book titles account for the lion's share of the use and a very large number of titles receive very little use (Trueswell 1965; Anderson 2006). Figure 1.1 reproduces one of Trueswell's 1965 graphs.

The 1979 study at the University of Pittsburgh reported that 40 percent of books did not circulate during the first six years after purchase, and thereafter the likelihood of use plummeted to one in fifty. This study also included what we now recognize as a classic long tail graph (Bulick, Sabar, and Flynn 1979, 9–18).

The findings of these and other use studies of books were alarming. Did the results mean that librarians were not fulfilling their collection development responsibilities very well? Should materials budgets be slashed because only a fraction of the collection met users' needs? (Sargent 1979, 416).

University faculty and librarians alike were quick to point out flaws in both the methodologies and interpretations of the findings of these and other circulation use study reports that have been conducted over the years. Voigt expressed concern that the research habits of faculty and advanced graduate students are very different from the circulation habits of undergraduates (Voigt 1979, 66). Some authors wrote that in-house use, especially by faculty and graduate students, can be high and, if these patrons reshelve material themselves, these uses are never captured in circulation studies (Borkowski and MacLeod 1979; Harris 1977; Stockard, Griffin, and Coblyn 1979). Other writers pointed out that not all circulations are created equal because the extent of *actual* use by patrons may vary widely. The same argument can be made for in-library use; there is a big difference between a user flipping through ten books before selecting one to check out, and a user who takes a book to a library desk and spends all afternoon reading it. Harris called the former a "useless use" and the latter a "serious" use (Harris 1977). Since these differences can never be detected (except in a few isolated cases), most librarians conducting use studies simply make the assumption that all uses

FIGURE 1.1

Trueswell's 1965 "Long Tail" Graph

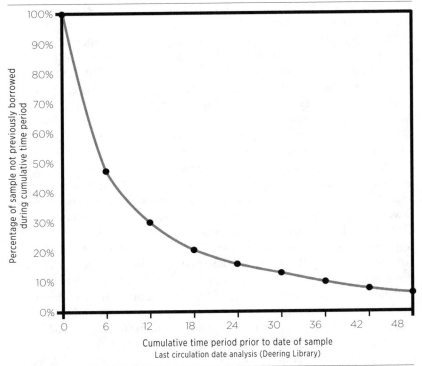

Cumulative time period prior to date of sample
Last circulation date analysis (Deering Library)

SOURCE: Trueswell, Richard W. 1965. "A Quantitative Measure of User Circulation Requirements and Its Possible Effect on Stack Thinning and Multiple Copy Determination." *American Documentation* 16 (1): 21. Copyright © 1965 Wiley Periodicals, Inc., A Wiley Company. Permission to reproduce granted by Wiley.

are indeed equal, or at least average out (Broadus 1980, 323). In a number of studies that analyzed multiple years of circulation data, some books were present during the entire period under examination, whereas others were added partway through; critics pounced on the fact that not all books had the same chance for use and thus the results must be skewed.

Hardesty suggested that although "recorded circulation figures do not adequately measure the research uses of a university library, recorded circulation statistics may be more appropriate for measuring the undergraduate use of a college library" (Hardesty 1981, 262). He replicated the Pittsburgh study at a small liberal arts college and found that 44 percent of the books in his study had not circulated during the first three years after entering the collection and 37 percent did not circulate during an entire five-year period. He concluded that the books in his study "displayed a general pattern of little or no use, and a small number accounted for a majority of the total use," a pattern very similar to Trueswell's 80/20 rule. In addition, the books in this study also followed the Pittsburgh pattern of newly acquired books exhibiting a steep decline in circulation once they had been in the collection more than three years (Hardesty 1981, 266).

Eldredge replicated Trueswell's study in a health sciences library. Although he found that the 80/20 rule was actually 80/38 in this library, he agreed that his results confirmed "previous observations that a certain vital few monographs in a collection will experience disproportionately heavy circulation demand" (Eldredge 1998, 499). Eldredge also raised the question of the ratio of users to books, suggesting that a smaller collection serving a proportionately larger number of users will inevitably show different circulation patterns than a larger collection and smaller group of users.

The underlying theme in all these studies is that a high percentage of material purchased for academic library collections is seldom or never used. In case librarians are tempted to dismiss these decades-old circulation studies, it is worth mentioning a few recent studies that confirm the same trends. Cornell University Library's 2010 circulation study found that 55 percent of the books acquired since 1990 had never circulated (*Report of the Collection Development Executive Committee* 2010, 2). A 2009 study at Purdue University Libraries reported that 33 percent of librarian-selected books acquired between 2000 and 2009 had not circulated; the same study also reported that patron-selected books acquired through interlibrary loan's buy-on-demand program circulated at a significantly higher rate (Nixon and Saunders 2010, 156–57).

It is also worth noting that according to the annual statistics gathered by the Association of Research Libraries, even university libraries with large and renowned collections borrow tens of thousands of items every year (many of them books), which suggests that Hardesty was right when he remarked that "the problem may not be that too many books are being acquired, but that the wrong books are being acquired" (Kyrillidou, Morris, and Roebuck 2012, 98; Hardesty 1981, 272). Britten determined that Trueswell's 80/20 rule applied to his own large research library's circulation patterns, but when he examined circulation performance in various LC classifications against the collection's overall performance, he identified a number of high-performance areas. He suggested rewarding high-use areas with a larger percentage of the collections budget so that they could be expanded to meet demonstrated user need (Britten 1990, 189).

Use studies, however they are formulated, generally conclude that "use is a predictor of [more] use, though that use does generally decline over the years" (Broadus 1980, 322). For this reason, librarians treat low use and no use as major factors when selecting books to move to storage facilities or to withdraw. Not everyone agrees with this conclusion, however; Eldredge wrote that "past usage patterns have limited relevance to predicting future patterns," and further wondered "whether customers are actually satisfied with what they check out" (Eldredge 1998, 502).

Sargent reviewed a small sample of little-used books at a medium-sized college library serving mainly undergraduates. He found that most of these books fit into one of four categories: irrelevant (which applied to only a few); out-of-fashion art and literature; obsolete; and specialized (e.g., in-depth historical studies and technical books). He concluded that for almost all the books in the sample, the lack of use stemmed from "processes of change—the growth of knowledge and shifts in taste and interest—that are beyond the control of the library" (Sargent 1979, 420–22). In other words, Sargent felt that most of the books had originally been good choices based on the library's collection policy, but that time had eroded their usefulness.

There are many reasons why a large percentage of faculty-selected or librarian-selected titles seldom or never circulate. Research libraries attempt to collect comprehensively in some subject areas; inevitably users will find some of the material of more interest than others. There is a tacit understanding in these cases that comprehensive collecting inevitably results in some percentage of low-use material, and that this is acceptable. Britten remarked that "a high level of disuse can be said to be the price of scholarly potential" (Britten 1990, 188). However, Broadus, also affiliated with a large research institution, concluded that "no library should try to be complete for any community of users. If it is, it apparently will have to collect and store thousands or millions of items that will be used once a decade or even less frequently" (Broadus 1980, 319).

There are other factors that might skew use studies. For example, in the past some libraries accepted many gift books, bloating their collections with donated titles that were not carefully selected, and that, in many cases, nobody used. Large numbers of untouched gift books will affect the outcome of use studies. Although he had accepted older gift books specifically "to strengthen the historical perspective" of his health sciences library, Eldredge purposely eliminated these books from his use study (Eldredge 1998, 497).

Circulation figures do not tell the whole story, of course. The act of checking out a book does not mean that the book will actually be used and, even if it is, librarians do not know how much it was used. There is always some in-house use that will never be captured, even in those studies designed to account for this factor by counting unshelved books left on library tables and in the photocopier area. Use studies will never generate completely accurate data, but they are the best indicators available. If librarians look at a last recorded use from fifteen or twenty years ago as part of a retention decision point, for example, it will be a relatively reliable marker that the book has little relevance for current users and probably very little for most future potential users, either.

The most common reason for low use is that for decades (or for centuries, in some cases), librarians or faculty selected books that they judged would meet the needs of their user populations; their patrons, however, only used a small subset, even when the titles were newly acquired. Why do patrons use only a relatively small percentage of titles from shelves of books on the Civil War or aeronautics or Spanish literature? Why, despite the availability of hundreds of titles about medieval Europe or bridge design or child development, do patrons request yet more titles on these subjects through interlibrary loan? Why can't the librarians get it right? Perhaps it just boils down to the fact that no matter how many books we buy on any topic, patrons find references to other ones that appear to be better matches to meet the need of the moment. Decades and centuries of acquiring millions of books that hardly anyone uses (even when new) should have taught us that it is impossible to predict future need, and thus future use, with any degree of certainty. Yet, like inveterate gamblers, we believe that we will get it right the next time, and once again go out and buy another shelf's worth of books even though the odds are that only a very few will be winners in the circulation lottery.

Should we blame our predecessors for buying all these books that no one uses and that we must now figure out what to do with what one librarian referred to as the "deadwood" ("Ridding Collections" 1989, 3)? We must remember that, until relatively recently, librarians bought many newly published books because if they delayed too long, the titles would go out of print and become both very hard to identify and expensive to purchase on the used book market. In the past, just as we often do today, librarians exercised their best professional judgment and bought the books that they thought their users would need. But then, as now, patrons did not select as many of the books as the librarians thought they would, or used some of them only when they were new and then stopped consulting them. One reason why some librarians resist the idea of rightsizing is that they wonder if all those low- and no-use books are mute reminders of their collection development "mistakes." However, many of these past acquisitions are unused today because they have outlived their usefulness, not because they were poor choices.

One part of rightsizing academic library collections is dealing with the buildup of unused material, but another part involves changing our collection development behavior so that we do not perpetuate the same old model in the virtual environment. Centuries of building collections using the just-in-case model have resulted in academic libraries overflowing with titles that received little use when they were newly published, millions of which now languish in stacks and storage facilities. And, in an ironic twist, hundreds of copies of these exact same titles sit unused in hundreds of libraries.

CHANGING ENVIRONMENT

Many recent changes within the academy, the publishing industry, and libraries themselves have begun to affect the size and nature of library collections and the space used to house them.

Recent revolutionary changes in publishing, distribution channels, and technology have reshaped the landscape for scholarly and technical publications. The concept of material going out of print may soon be obsolete for most mainstream publications. With the rise of electronic copies and print-on-demand services, most titles will be available in either digital or print form at any point in the foreseeable future. There is diminishing need to buy today in case a user might need a title tomorrow, because now purchase and delivery can occur quickly, and often seamlessly, at the moment when a user expresses an interest in a title. Patron-driven acquisition (PDA) plans allow academic libraries to put tens of thousands of e-book titles into their catalogs and discovery layers where users can find them easily; the library pays for them only when patrons use them. Librarians today should seriously question the need for floods of titles to arrive via approval plans. Unfortunately, many librarians find it difficult to break decades of just-in-case acquisitions habits; they now frequently buy e-books outright rather than fully embracing the just-in-time patron-driven acquisitions model which defers purchase until the moment of need which, for thousands of titles, may never come.

Librarians now also grapple with significant declines in circulation. There are several explanations for this trend, the most notable being that users tend to look for digital information first, whether it be electronic resources acquired by the library or information found on the Internet. Although for the foreseeable future some information will only be available in a printed format, not only will that amount dwindle over time, but also potential users of that information will become increasingly likely to accept digital substitutes for the sake of speed and convenience, even if the quality is not always as good or as reliable as print.

Interlibrary loan services have become more and more automated over the past few years. Delivery of many articles and chapters to users' desktops may only take a day or two, a time period almost indistinguishable from the time needed to supply scanned articles from the institution's own print copies. Academic libraries usually belong to at least one or two consortial groups that have negotiated fast delivery of physical items among members, and generally a very high percentage of ILL requests for physical items can be filled by partner libraries. As of this writing, the possibility of being able to lend an acceptable version of an e-book while complying with licensing agreements is nearing reality. In addition, many academic interlibrary loan units have added on-demand purchase options into their workflow: should a local patron request a book that meets certain predetermined criteria (e.g., published within an established time frame, under a certain price threshold, scholarly in nature), the staff often buys it either in an e-book or print book edition from a vendor that delivers it quickly. This practice meets not only the requesting user's need, but also those of future users, because the book will be added to the library's collection after the first patron's use. Studies conducted since these plans have been in place (generally from about 2000 onward) have shown that books purchased in this way enjoy higher subsequent use than similar librarian-selected titles (Nixon and Saunders 2010; Tyler et al. 2010).

Major changes over the past few years are making the buy-and-hold-for-all-eternity model obsolete for all but the largest research libraries. With central campus space at a premium, some libraries have already downsized their physical footprint, often as a result of decisions by campus administration. This is generally accomplished by reducing the physical collection size and repurposing some stacks area for other uses, such as group-study spaces, learning commons areas, and computer workstations. Other libraries may close subject branch locations and assimilate those collections into already-crowded stacks in larger locations, which may necessitate a multiyear weeding project to create more room. Libraries lucky enough to have storage facilities may find them filling up at an alarming rate as the active collections downsize for various reasons. Little's 2013 survey article calls this scramble for more or repurposed space "The Space Race" (Little 2013, 351).

"Ownership versus access" became a catch phase in the 1980s, when librarians began to rely more heavily on being able to borrow material that their own libraries did not own from library partners. Improvements in consortial partnerships, telecommunications, and delivery options all played their part in the dramatic increase of interlibrary loan services. With the recent explosion of digital content, a library's patrons can now access far more material than ever, because most libraries also "own" a growing mass of material that they never held in physical form.

One question that the wary or reluctant sometimes ask is, "What will our physical library collection look like if most of our new material is digital and most of the older material is only accessible in collaborative storage facilities located miles away?" One translation for this question is, "What will collections librarians do in this new world?" Collections librarians' changing roles will include participating in "regional and eventually national preservation and access partnerships, . . . gathering print materials from countries without strong archival programs," and building "local, unusual, specialized, and unique materials as their primary focus" (Kieft and Payne 2012, 138). Managing the various aspects of access to digital material requires specialized skills. Digitizing, describing, and making accessible local copies of rare and unique material will increase in importance. Library resources will "support a large-scale, integrated approach to preserving and giving access to print and digital publications . . . rather than on housing general collection print materials locally" (Kieft and Payne 2012, 141). Time that librarians once devoted to title-by-title selection can be repurposed to other areas, such as information literacy, getting involved in the research process with teaching faculty, engaging in scholarly communication activities, becoming more deeply involved in liaison roles with the academic departments, and taking advantage of other new opportunities as they present themselves in the years ahead (Bracke, Hérubel, and Ward 2010).

Academic librarians often bemoan the fact that it is becoming harder to attract patrons, especially the younger ones, to the library for any reason other than finding a place to study. We tell ourselves that digital collections appeal more to the "net generation," and wonder how to make the "library as place" more important in the students' academic lives. Have we paused long enough to consider that we might attract more users (as opposed to sitters) if our physical collections were uncluttered, attractive, relevant, and easy to navigate?

Librarians have cooperated in many ways with consortia or other libraries in their regions for decades. Sharing material via interlibrary loan is a major form of this. Libraries have more recently experimented with group purchasing plans; one particularly successful example of this cooperation is the work undertaken to negotiate group deals to buy electronic products across a consortium, state, or region in "big deal" arrangements. Some libraries have worked together for years on group storage projects, typically building and maintaining joint facilities or establishing a facility and inviting other local libraries to participate by depositing material for a fee. Collaborative storage plans coupled with print reduction projects are on the rise and will be explored in a later section.

2
Traditional Deselection Solutions

W EEDING, OR ANY OF THE OTHER TERMS LIBRARIANS USE FOR permanently removing material from the shelves, has had a checkered past in academic libraries.

Public libraries and smaller academic libraries routinely face and deal with this issue. They have limited public shelf space and usually do not have access to significant amounts of storage space. Because their missions and goals differ from those of larger academic libraries, it is more appropriate for them to provide titles that are mainly of current interest to their user populations and to supplement their offerings with interlibrary loan services and, more recently, with some combination of buy-on-demand services, patron-driven e-book acquisitions plans, or e-book subscription programs. In general, the number of incoming print books must be offset by a similar number of departing books. Public libraries often have annual or biennial processes in place for routine weeding projects, usually based on circulation statistics. Although the content of their collections changes, their size remains relatively constant.

Larger academic and research libraries have different missions and different user communities. Besides building a solid collection for undergraduates, they also support students at the master's and doctoral levels, as well as faculty who conduct everything from cutting edge scientific research to in-depth studies on historical subjects. For decades, librarians at these libraries served their clientele not only by buying the works that they judged their users would need for their current learning and research interests, but also by maintaining all or almost all the books that they and their predecessors had bought in the past, often going back a century or more. Until fairly recently, librarians at research institutions probably assumed that they would maintain nearly every title acquired. When space became a challenge, librarians often divided the collection between "a low-use storage area and a high-use core area" (Trueswell 1976, 79).

A few of the very largest research libraries can limit their weeding activities to withdrawing damaged or worn-out books or reducing the number of multiple copies of older titles. They have both the mandate and the funds to keep nearly every item they have ever acquired, if not in the circulating collection, then in massive storage facilities. Because of their reputations, their budgets, and in many cases their long histories, they also have a higher percentage of unique or scarce material; they also are serious about their responsibility to preserve and maintain these items not only for their own scholars, but also for those at other institutions who plan to visit or borrow the material.

Most academic libraries, however, do not fall into this top echelon. Although each has some unique or scarce material, such as local theses, dissertations, research reports, faculty papers, or local or regional publications, the vast majority of their titles are widely duplicated elsewhere. Because of this, many academic libraries have undertaken weeding projects over the years, although not always in routine, systematic, ongoing, and systemwide ways. Rather, these sporadic weeding projects frequently addressed only the need to relieve crowding in specific areas of the stacks or to absorb the collection of a small branch library into a larger location. Librarians conducted weeding projects in different libraries on the same campus in different ways, at different times, and with different criteria. Weeding was often regarded as a distasteful, last-resort activity, undertaken reluctantly and finished with a sigh of relief that it need not occur again for a long time.

Traditional weeding is a labor-intensive process. Even if librarians set up the criteria or guidelines and then direct the support staff to do most of the volume pulling, records maintenance, and material disposal, time must still be spent reviewing titles to be sure that the library retains scarce or valuable titles, books related to the local institution or the region, or a few journal titles whose content does not reproduce well in electronic format. Some of the many articles published in the past that described weeding methodology described laborious title-by-title volume checks at the shelves, putting questionnaire slips into withdrawal candidates and checking them months later for any patron comments, placing paper into volumes in such a way that later inspection would reveal in-house use, checking titles against standard bibliographies so that librarians could keep the "good" books, or pulling hundreds of books off the shelves for review elsewhere and then reshelving up to half of them. "The time required for the librarians to review the titles was greater than anticipated" is the first sentence in the section titled "Problems Encountered" in one article (Reed and Erickson 1993, 178).

CRITERIA FOR WEEDING

In the past, librarians had several options for approaching weeding.

Withdrawals Based on Superseded Volumes

Perhaps the easiest weeding decisions are those based on superseded volumes. Although a title is being discarded, it has been replaced by one that is more up-to-date, so in effect the content remains accessible in updated form.

Librarians routinely keep reference collections current by removing older editions when new ones appear. Of course, they often simply transfer the older editions to the circulating stacks or to a storage facility, thus contributing to the overall challenge of shelves crowded with unused titles. In numerous cases, withdrawing a superseded edition would have been a far better decision than relegating it another part of the library where it would sit untouched for decades. How many times, for example, will anyone consult the 1972 edition of the *Encyclopedia of Associations* when the most recent edition is available? Today librarians buy many reference works in electronic form, but how often do they check the print reference collection or storage stacks to remove obsolete print editions?

Textbooks for reserve collections are also candidates for systematic withdrawal. When the 8th edition of *Introduction to Economics* arrives, for example, out goes the 7th edition. Books that are not obviously textbooks and that are shelved in the stacks may not receive the same routine weeding treatment, so newer editions join their predecessors.

Should all older editions be routinely discarded? Making a blanket pronouncement on the question of editions is unwise. There are often reasons to keep the current two, five, or ten years of some titles (sometimes split between the reference and circulating collections), whereas other titles should be kept indefinitely. For example, before the availability of the electronic version, institutions with engineering and technology programs might have decided to retain each edition of the *Annual Book of ASTM Standards* and its accompanying index, despite the fact that it ran to dozens of volumes each year and only a small percentage of the standards were revised annually. It may be critical for an engineer or lawyer to have quick access to decades-old standards for bolts, ladders, concrete, insulation, and so on.

Withdrawals Based on Low Circulation

Withdrawing books based on low circulation is a time-honored method. Fifty or more years ago, a typical summer project at an academic library might have been designating a section of the stacks and opening every book to the due date slip; if there was no evidence of checkout activity after a certain date, the books went onto carts for a final review by a librarian before being de-accessioned. A decade or so after the advent of automated circulation systems, it was possible to generate lists of low- and no-circulation books so that staff could pull titles from a pick list. Librarians might review the pick lists before staff pulled books, or might review carts or workroom shelves afterwards. Librarians at large institutions also used this process to identify books to transfer to storage facilities. The work was described as "physically exhausting and often dirty" as well as harder to do during fall and spring semesters "when other activities intensified," and while wearing professional attire (Dubicki 2008, 134). Searching the literature reveals dozens of now-obsolete articles about methods librarians used in pre- and early-automation days to weed their book collections based on low use. Today, circulation statistics are still a part of the process for identifying withdrawal candidates, but they are now only one of a wide array of factors that librarians take into account (as will be explored in chapter 3).

Gathering journal usage statistics for print volumes was always a cumber-some and time-consuming process. Many libraries' policies did not allow journals to be checked out, so no circulation statistics were routinely captured. Usage figures could only be generated by staff making reshelving notes for pieces left on tables or near photocopy machines. Some libraries constantly monitored usage, while others sampled it during a few random weeks each year or only conducted journal-use studies when required for projects like serials cuts. This method introduced many of the same limitations of trying to determine in-house use of books that have been previously enumerated, complicated further because it was impossible to tell if users had consulted more than one article in an issue or volume.

In the past, librarians approached the issue of weeding journals (or can-celling them or sending them to a storage facility) very differently than they do today. Low use, or as one author described it, "item consultation decay rate," was a possible variable, but since it was so difficult to determine use of noncirculating items, the process often involved sophisticated analyses of multiple variables that included assessing some combination of other factors including the half-life of the literature, a journal's age, citation analysis, cita-tion impact factor, price, where titles were indexed, language, accreditation requirements, relation to the curriculum, interlibrary loan statistics, length of the run, literature growth rate, regional availability, publishers' reputations, and declining publishing output of faculty in specialized areas. Articles on this topic were often accompanied by complicated graphs and formulas (Brookes 1970; Burton and Kebler 1960; Cole 1963; Line 1970, Sandison 1971; Seymour 1972b; Stankus 1986). Several articles pointed out flaws in the methodology or philosophy of previously published works. Segal's 1986 review provides a helpful summary of methods employed up until the time it was written (Segal 1986). Whatever the evaluation process, it would require manual calculations and likely would be very time-consuming and thus costly to employ, especially when factoring faculty input into the equation. In addition, most of these studies examined engineering and scientific literature, which is generally acknowledged to have a relatively short useful life (although some articles may be cited for decades). For example, Fleming and Kilgour reported that 80 percent of the journal use in two academic health-sciences libraries could be attributed to 28 percent of the titles (Fleming and Kilgour 1964). In the social sciences and humanities, however, many articles remain relevant for a very long time. Sandison made the point that lower citation rates for older articles do not necessarily mean that the content is obsolete; in other words, low use does not necessarily equate to low value (Sandison 1971, 184). The concept of value is subjective, however; nevertheless one wonders about the value of an article that no one consults, no matter how valid it may still be.

In the preelectronic past, withdrawing or cancelling a print journal was a very serious step for many reasons, not least of which because obtaining article copies from other libraries was a relatively slow process before electronic delivery arrived on the scene.

Withdrawals Based on Electronic Access

This option is a newer solution and plays a major role in rightsizing, but it may also be considered a traditional solution because librarians sometimes employ it in isolation from other potential rightsizing activities. Most withdrawals based on electronic access involve journals, because of the significant amount of shelf space that can be freed. Handled as a stand-alone project, these endeavors are usually confined to withdrawing duplicates, instead of as part of a big-picture rightsizing effort. However, there are often good reasons for embarking on such a project, or such a project may pave the way for a larger, more encompassing one. For details on how to undertake journal withdrawals based on electronic access, see chapter 4.

STORAGE

Many of the rightsizing techniques described in this book could be applied to identifying titles to transfer from central campus stacks to a storage facility. This book argues, however, that in many cases rightsizing the collection provides a better long-term solution for many libraries because, among other things, it avoids the cost of building, retrofitting, or maintaining a storage facility filled with low-use titles widely held elsewhere. However, many libraries already have a storage facility or may have very good reasons, despite rightsizing efforts, for building one, so it is helpful to mention storage options in the discussion.

This is also a good place to mention the distinction between *storing* an item and *preserving* it. Storing a library item means identifying it as a non-core title and moving it away from the active core collection; in other words, keeping it "just in case." If an item has some particular value, then the library wants to keep it in such a way as to maintain its condition, prevent damage, and provide long-term access to it for scholars, usually by identifying it as a title that will reside in a special collection under the care of archivists. Storage, which certainly keeps an item, provides access to it, makes reasonable efforts not to damage it, and makes no attempt to treat it with the same care as archival material. Some items that should be in special collections may in fact reside in storage; therefore the rightsizing methods described in chapter 3 are designed to protect scarce items or material of local interest from consideration for withdrawal.

Local Storage

A newly acquired title is likely to be recently published and therefore at the peak of its potential usefulness. In other words, it is an *asset*. The costs associated with shelving, circulating, and otherwise maintaining it are justified because it is being used or because the potential of use is relatively high. Over time, its potential usefulness typically dwindles; even if it was once at least potentially useful, over the years its content becomes obsolete or out of fashion. At some point what was once an asset becomes a *liability*, especially in terms of occupying space in an active and growing library collection.

Decades ago, when it was difficult to identify which other libraries held desired titles and borrowing them was a slow process, librarians wanted to keep these no- and low-use items in case someone needed them again, but also wanted to relieve stacks crowded with many such older items. Moving low-use volumes to an on-campus annex or to basement or attic storage is a time-honored tradition. Some libraries have so many local storage locations that their fragmented collections would put a squirrel to shame. Because pressure for reallocating space on a central campus has become acute, librarians must scramble, sometimes on short notice, to relocate these pockets of largely unused material. At the author's institution some years ago, one such annex needed to be cleared out for another purpose. Upon inquiry, it transpired that patrons only requested about three hundred books per year from this location—an average of less than one book per day from a collection of tens of thousands of volumes. Nevertheless, at that time the subject librarians were reluctant to weed the collection, so it was moved in its entirety to basement storage space in another building. These volumes have now been included in a library-wide rightsizing project.

At some point local storage no longer provides an adequate solution for housing low-use material. All available locations eventually reach capacity. The library or institution may want to convert at least some of the storage space for other functions. There may be an opportunity to retrofit a large building or warehouse as a central storage facility, or the administration may develop some other plan for centralized storage. In the past, storage facilities popped up like mushrooms at large- and medium-sized institutions, as the then-obvious solution to the ubiquitous challenge of managing endlessly growing physical collections. A high percentage of the same low- and no-use books were stored in each of these dozens of facilities.

Remote Storage

Remote storage generally refers to facilities that are not located on an institution's central campus. At some institutions, the term may refer to a facility on the edge of a main campus some distance from the active library locations. In other places, the remote storage facility may be located dozens of miles away.

Sometimes these storage facilities are retrofitted spaces that were originally built for other purposes, such as a disused warehouse miles from the central campus. Install some shelving and a security system, and make arrangements for periodic visits to page and reshelve material, and one has an instant library annex! Library material can be moved to the facility in large blocks. With a little organization, they can be shelved in any convenient order and retrieved via shelf location numbers noted in the updated catalog records, thus making optimal use of the shelving space. Although such a solution may be relatively inexpensive, it often places the collection at risk because of factors such as insufficient or nonexistent climate control, a leaky roof, or problems with rodents, insects, mold, or other hazards. Sometimes a processing and office area is created so that the facility can be staffed, and there may even be a small reading room for patrons who want to visit to consult large quantities of material. If staffed, personnel can fill most requests for journal articles and book chapters by scanning them and delivering them electronically for campus document fulfillment and interlibrary loan requests. Arrangements will still need to be made for physically moving some items to and from the storage facility on demand. It is also useful to have a procedure for repatriating an occasional higher-use title to the central campus collection.

In 2010, Courant and Nielson calculated that it cost 86 cents a year to maintain a book in a high-density storage facility versus $4.26 per book in an open-stack library (Courant and Nielson 2010, 91). Although these figures will change over time, the fact remains that storing a volume is significantly less expensive than maintaining it in an active collection. Rightsizing offers the further possibility of avoiding the costs associated with building or retrofitting a storage facility, or adding more seldom-consulted items to an existing facility. Of course, there are costs associated with rightsizing, but ideally they will be included in the cost of routine management of a physical collection. In addition, the costs of identifying, locating, and withdrawing an item are one-time costs, not ongoing ones.

The availability of seemingly vast areas of remote storage often encourages librarians to stifle any weeding impulses. It seems so much easier simply to move low-use material to a facility *en masse* rather than to take the time to evaluate it for potential withdrawal candidates or for items that should move to special collections. The "out of sight, out of mind" principle comes into play with little regard for the fact that should weeding eventually be undertaken, it will be far more difficult to manage the process in a storage facility where the shelving arrangement may be dictated by some combination of factors such as size or arrival date, rather than primarily by call number.

Earlier, the author used a gambling analogy to describe how librarians traditionally selected new material by using their best judgment, but essentially hoping that the books they acquired would be ones that patrons would use. So often, despite their best intentions, librarians get it wrong, and users never touch a high percentage of this material. It is interesting to note that librarians do an excellent job identifying material to send to storage—the vast majority of low- and no-use titles that they identify as no longer being relevant in the active collections move to storage and sit there undisturbed for decades. Many storage facilities see circulation rates of 2 percent or less per year. It should be an easy transition for librarians to channel their abilities for selecting the right items to store into strategies for identifying the right items to withdraw.

Many factors come into play when a library decides that a remote storage facility is the right move. One major factor is the nature of the particular university and its library. In the case of major research universities that may also serve as regional suppliers or consortial leaders, it may make perfect sense to build and maintain a state-of-the-art library storage facility containing virtually everything the library ever purchased that is not currently enjoying fairly high use. But for many libraries, the traditional solution of a storage facility may no longer be the one and only obvious answer to collection-space pressures on a central campus. Administrators must answer these questions honestly: Does our library really need to go to the expense of building and then maintaining for the foreseeable future a facility to house a large mass of low- and no-use library material that is for the most part widely held elsewhere and that is both easily and quickly obtainable through stable and reliable resource sharing arrangements? Do we really need to keep long runs of print journals when we have perpetual access to the electronic equivalents? Would it be more cost-effective to pay for occasional access from somewhere else for a relatively few titles than to pay ongoing costs for long-term local access to hundreds of thousands of readily available seldom-used titles?

One further point to consider is the possible difficulty of any future weeding from the storage facility itself. It is relatively easy to weed from a unit with compact shelving. Removing volumes from a high-density facility is another matter altogether. With ranges 30 feet high that can only be reached with hydraulic lift equipment, removing tens of thousands of volumes would be an enormous undertaking, as would keeping track of the bins from which volumes had been removed, all so that the bins could be later filled to capacity again with incoming material. Material that goes to a high-density facility usually does so with the understanding that it will remain there for the lifespan of the building. If the facility serves one of the top research universities, or if it is designed to serve regional or consortial members, then it makes sense to shelve all volumes of *Books in Print* since it began publication in 1948. However, librarians at a facility designed mainly to serve a local institution should think twice before storing this same run of volumes. The chance of local need for the volumes is very slim and they are readily available elsewhere through interlibrary loan should the need arise a few times in the next century.

Bravender and Long described a project to withdraw 14,000 items from one subject area in a central library's automated retrieval system, an arduous endeavor requiring volume-by-volume retrieval from automated book bins. They described the process as "cumbersome and time-consuming," especially because librarians wanted to examine most of the items before making a final withdrawal decision (Bravender and Long 2011, 243). Consider how much more cumbersome and time-consuming a project to remove ten times or more as many volumes from high-density remote storage would be.

Trueswell suggested that "there is some evidence that essentially the same titles will be found among the little-used books of most college libraries" (Trueswell 1976, 102). What seemed likely at the time of his 1976 article has been proven today by even a cursory examination of the huge national and international bibliographic databases. Hundreds of libraries bought huge aggregate quantities of the same books in the past. Even if some of them were heavily used when they were new, hundreds of copies of the same titles now languish unused in storage facilities and on crowded active shelves. Future demand for them will in many cases be very low, and could be easily met by a handful of copies held in storage facilities across a region or country.

For most institutions, any kind of storage used as a warehousing function, whether local or remote, merely defers the problem and buys time. "The underlying problem remains. There are too many books. There are too many copies of the same books. And there are too many unused books to justify the space they now occupy, and the time spent caring for them" (Lugg and Fischer 2008b, 88).

Some libraries have participated for years in collaborative storage solutions with nearby or peer institutions. For them, collaborative storage solutions are a traditional way of addressing overcrowding or obsolescence in active collections. Chapter 3 discusses collaborative storage and print retention options that may be newer options for many libraries. These facilities offer both adequate and more affordable alternatives to building and maintaining new single-institution remote storage facilities.

MOVING BEYOND WEEDING AND STORAGE

What do all of these traditional solutions have in common? They are usually slow, cumbersome, expensive, and tedious to implement. They generally involve title-by-title review. Some solutions involve retaining low-use material by moving it to other locations where the library must still pay to maintain it, albeit at lower costs than in central-campus space. Librarians often apply traditional solutions to small parts of the collection rather than to the collection as a whole.

There are only two reasons why this process is likely to decrease of its own accord in the coming decades. First, some libraries will weed or store or both to the point where their central physical collection is a lean and relatively active core one. Second, as libraries acquire more and more digital content, there will be less and less newly acquired print that will morph, a few decades later, into low- or no-use print.

Why do librarians keep material that has never or seldom been used, or material that was used when relatively new, but now no longer interests users—especially when those titles are widely held elsewhere and easily obtainable through interlibrary loan? Why are retention issues fraught with peril in libraries, whereas campus scientists routinely discard older or obsolete equipment without a qualm and without arousing passionately negative feelings in others?

Academic librarians have been trained in school and practice to maintain the venerable tradition of preserving the intellectual record. They regard collection building as a sacred trust and devote considerable energy and attention to careful description and organization of the material consigned to their care. Library budgets are tight; librarians also have a thrifty gene that makes them unwilling to discard items bought with precious dollars in previous years. In addition, the librarians whom we ask today to make retention decisions are often the same people who have spent the past few decades of their professional lives selecting the very items that are now candidates for withdrawal.

Their commitment to patron service struggles with the dilemma of occasionally asking a patron to wait a few days to receive an older book through interlibrary loan, versus maintaining tens or hundreds of thousands of books locally for faster access on those few occasions when one is needed. There may also be some concern that discarding books that no one has touched in the past quarter-century will result in faculty marching on the administration building in protest. In short, for a variety of reasons, it is difficult for some of our colleagues to start making the transition from the centuries-old just-in-case library collection model to the newer just-in-time paradigm.

To address the many interconnected factors discussed earlier about changes affecting academic library services, librarians must face the challenge of figuring out how to reduce the footprint of physical collections effectively. Using traditional solutions is no longer necessarily the best or only approach. New solutions offer ways to manage massive print retention projects that maximize effectiveness while minimizing distress.

3
Rightsizing Solutions

OME TRADITIONAL SOLUTIONS ARE STILL EFFECTIVE FOR
small-scale situations addressing the challenge of library spaces crowded
with physical items, but in many libraries, it is just not feasible for librarians
to spend years making volume-by-volume retention decisions based in large
part on individual inspection. Today there are automated, data-driven batch
methods for approaching the situation, especially on a large scale. The rightsizing solution calls for a withdrawal policy, a written plan, and methods that help
librarians identify large numbers of no- and low-use items that can be withdrawn relatively quickly and without harming the overall collection integrity.

This chapter provides a discussion of rightsizing solutions. For details on
operationalizing them, see chapter 4.

THE WITHDRAWAL POLICY

Although having a withdrawal policy may not be a new solution for many
libraries, it is important to stress that a library embarking on a rightsizing
plan should have a current withdrawal policy in place, either as part of the

selection or collection development policy or as a separate document. Not only is having the policy part of good general library management, but it is also helpful to have the policy formally approved by the relevant authorities and posted on the library's website. Some degree of potential opposition (both internal and external) may be deflected if the policy and the rationale behind it are easily accessible. For example, one library explains the weeding rationale as "Weeding is important in keeping a vibrant, relevant, effective, and accurate library collection. It is necessary for removing outdated or misinformation from the collection. . . . It makes the available materials more visible and accessible which could result in increased circulation of materials" (Northeastern State 2014). Even library staff and users who understand the need for occasional small weeding projects may find it helpful to review the reasons for larger rightsizing activities.

Several authors have addressed the topic of weeding policies. Stueart pointed out that a "collection retirement policy" is just as vital to "assure continued quality in the collection" as a collection development policy (Stueart 1985, 49). Pidgeon mentioned that a deselection policy "provides some institutional memory on what may have been done in the past and provides guidelines that ensure consistency from year to year" (Pidgeon 1995, 68). Handis suggested that a good collection development policy states not only the criteria for both collecting and discarding, but also "protects librarians in times of trouble" (Handis 2007, 85). "Protect" may not be quite the right word; the fallout after a horrified faculty member complains to the provost may be unpleasant, but it helps if the posted collection development policy clearly states the library's criteria for both acquisition and retention and if the provost already knows about the scale of the rightsizing project before receiving the complaint. Handis went on to describe how his library director "was responsible for getting [the policy] approved by upper-level administration. This was important since approval from the administration makes it clear how the library plans to proceed" (Handis 2007, 85). Another library includes this statement in its Weeding/Discard Procedures: "If faculty members disagree with specific discard decisions, the Assistant Dean for Collection Development will consider those disagreements. The librarian who recommended discarding the disputed item will not be identified without his or her consent" (Auburn University 2011).

As with any library policy, the withdrawal policy should be reviewed and updated periodically.

THE RIGHTSIZING PLAN

Developing a rightsizing plan implies that library administrators recognize the importance of taking a long, hard look at the physical collection, making decisions about what material should be removed, and then carrying out the plan within a certain time frame. Developing the plan means producing a document that states the project's goals, importance, and priority; makes it clear who has the responsibility and authority to act to carry it out from the planning phase through to action and completion; and cements the administration's commitment by identifying and providing adequate resources. While developing the plan, the administration also identifies the person who will function as the project manager and involves him or her with the planning process.

The rightsizing plan need not be longer than a few pages, but it should clearly state the project's objectives, staffing assignments, available resources, importance and relationship to the library's primary goals, expected time frame for a large retroactive effort, measures of success, and strategy for ongoing maintenance. The plan acknowledges that although the first phase of the project may be a large one that addresses the results of decades during which collections grew without periodic retention reviews, the administration makes a commitment to ongoing or at least periodic future reviews. "Weeding is not a special event; rather it is an integral part of the lifecycle management of content. The goal is no longer to build a larger collection; the goal is to assure that content most likely to be used is onsite, and that space for users continues to take precedence over inert content" (Lugg and Fischer 2009, 76).

Library administrators making the decision to embark on a rightsizing project should take the time to articulate the project objectives. Typically these objectives will be one or more of the following:

- repurposing existing library space
- maximizing the potential of new library space
- relieving pressure in current storage facilities or avoiding the cost of building or expanding one
- improving users' ability to find current and relevant material
- removing material, particularly journals, for which the electronic equivalent is readily available
- collaborating with library consortial partners in a cooperative print retention plan

As with any project, a print retention project requires careful and thoughtful planning before the action stage. The planning period provides time for the leaders and major participants to think through and articulate the project's goals and objectives, to marshal the resources needed for successful completion, and to establish the criteria by which the project's success will be measured.

One of the first decisions is whether the rightsizing project will focus on books, journals, or both. If both, will they be handled consecutively (if so, which one first?) or simultaneously? Where does other material like microform or audiovisual titles fit into the mix?

Another early decision involves deciding if the library will act on its own, or as a member of a group. A library need not, and in fact should not, make all its print retention decisions in a vacuum, based only on its own holdings and circulation records. A single library should compare its holdings to those of its consortial partners or to other libraries and make decisions accordingly. However, the option now exists to conduct print retention projects among multiple libraries, such as those in a consortium of similar-sized institutions or in a statewide cooperative. There are even examples of successful group projects among libraries of considerably different sizes, or projects by groups that include some large public libraries.

One question that inevitably arises during the objectives-setting phase is whether there is a target number of volumes, titles, or linear feet to be removed and, if so, will the target be applied across the entire collection or by subject area or location?

To explore this question, let's take the hypothetical example of a library that has 850,000 book volumes in four active collections: a main library (housing 500,000 books) and three branches. One branch, with 50,000 books, must close because the university administration plans to demolish the century-old building in which it is housed and use the site to build a new facility with modern classrooms and laboratories. There is no local storage facility and no plans to build one. The immediate task is to deal with the 50,000 books in the branch library. Circulation and catalog records reveal that 15,000 of them are either duplicated elsewhere in the system or have not circulated within the past fifteen years; these can be discarded (after first checking to be sure that none are scarce titles), leaving 35,000 books that must be absorbed by the main library. Do the librarians set a target of weeding 35,000 books from the main library (or, more wisely, 40,000 to 45,000 books to allow for some future growth) to accommodate this influx, or do they take this opportunity to embark on a rightsizing project for the books in the closing branch and the main library? Why not include the other two branches for a comprehensive view of the entire book collection?

The temptation, especially under pressure, is to meet the immediate goal of making enough room in the main library to absorb those books whose circulation history warrant retention. Even if this is the case, it is important to specify how that target will be reached. Using this example, if 45,000 books (9 percent) must be removed from the main library's collection, how will the librarians approach this task? There are a number of possibilities.

The multiple wave approach. Librarians might first remove duplicate copies, then sweep the stacks to remove books in poor condition, next identify older editions to discard, then remove any books for which the library now holds electronic versions, and finally replace some print books by buying electronic editions. The librarians may be lucky enough to remove a total of 45,000 books after having conducted all these activities, thus making room for the branch's books. This approach is not only very time-consuming, but also very timid and tentative. It preserves the just-in-case collection by removing very little unused content. It may in fact perpetuate the just-in-case collection by, among other things, going to the expense of replacing unused print books with their electronic counterparts, which will in all likelihood also not be used much.

No- and low-circulation approach. The librarians determine from querying their online circulation records that 129,000 (almost 26 percent) of the main library's 500,000 titles were acquired at least ten years ago and have either zero circulations or only a single circulation that occurred five or more years ago. This number is well over the target. Should the query be run again using only zero circulations as the major variable, even though the librarians have already agreed that one circulation five or more years old adequately indicates titles of very little interest or value to the user population? Do the librarians determine a way to remove a portion of the books on the list from each major classification area to reach the target of 45,000 weeded books across the collection? Or does weeding start systematically at the beginning of the collection and simply stop when 45,000 books have been removed? Do the librarians consciously skip any classifications for subjects in which the teaching faculty are known to be more vocal about the potential removal of titles? This approach is better than the first option in that it is based on use analysis and agreed-upon criteria, but it is still not quite rightsizing because the librarians want to stop after reaching the target.

The rightsizing approach. Using the approach advocated in this book, the librarians could take a rules-based look at all the books in the closing branch and in the main library (and possibly even in the two unaffected branches so that the entire system's collection benefits from an in-depth analysis) to determine which books no longer meet the needs of the user population and, based on no use at all or on no recent use, can be removed without harming the collection. A true rightsizing approach, as described in this book, includes factors such as considering titles in formats other than print (e.g., microform) and taking into account titles that may be the last copy in the state, region, or consortium, or that may be relatively scarce in the library community as a whole. Including all the collections in a library system (except special collections) involves all librarians and avoids the friction that might potentially arise if some branches or subjects face reductions of their collection and others do not. Rightsizing is not just about space management; it is also about honing a collection to make it more relevant and accessible for users.

Although there may be a good reason to set a target and stick to it, the initial impetus to reduce a physical collection offers the possibility of doing more than simply meeting a target to achieve a short-term goal. Savvy librarians leverage the need for a short-term collection-reduction project into a wakeup call to assess the entire collection (or at least a large part of it). The tools are available today to conduct these assessments by querying local electronic records or, for a broader assessment that takes into account the holdings of other relevant libraries, by hiring a consultant.

Having a target can be useful, however, if a certain amount of the collection must be removed for a remodeling imperative. If the number of withdrawal candidates is too low after the initial analysis, then librarians adjust the criteria so that the results of the next analysis encompass more titles. Simply meeting the target should not be the project's main driver, nor should it be the sole criterion of success.

Articulating and communicating the project goals and objectives help others, such as colleagues, staff, and university administrators and faculty, understand the reasons and importance of the rightsizing plan.

RULES-BASED MASS BOOK WITHDRAWALS

Before automation, book withdrawal projects were slow and cumbersome. They often involved staff opening books one by one to examine characteristics such as the publication date, the book's physical condition, and the number of stamps on the due date slips, while simultaneously scanning the shelf to determine which titles had duplicate copies or were part of a set. Even if the initial work was assigned to support staff who followed written guidelines, librarians usually reviewed the items selected to discard. Carts of books next traveled through the technical services department, where staff withdrew the records by removing catalog cards and shelflist cards and then disposed of the books (either to a library book sale or to bins destined for trash disposal (Reusch 1990). Identifying titles to move to a storage facility followed similar procedures, except that records were changed to show a new location and books were transferred instead of being discarded. Journal withdrawal projects were even more time-consuming; these required some determination of use over time for long periodical runs; this information was difficult and tedious to acquire because journals often did not circulate and thus their use was not automatically captured.

Today, few libraries have the time to conduct such painstaking reviews. Many find themselves in situations that require them to make retention decisions for significant portions of their collections within relatively short time frames. Many decisions must be made without opening a single book. This can be accomplished with rules-based batch-processing in which a computer algorithm assesses multiple factors about thousands of titles and produces a list of withdrawal candidates based on criteria thresholds developed by the librarians.

Lugg and Fischer pointed out that in recent decades most academic libraries' collections were built in large part on approval plans, whereby the collection grew by automatically adding titles that met the criteria of the librarian-crafted profile developed to match a book jobber's inventory. They suggested that rules-based weeding projects can be viewed as "disapproval plans" in which a librarian-crafted profile is applied to the collection so that disposition decisions (keep, store, withdraw) are made in batch mode, which is far more efficient than title-by-title reviews. Their article outlines an approach to building candidate lists that includes decision points for many factors, including ineligible titles (e.g., in special collections or in certain call number ranges), circulation parameters, key words (e.g., the library's home state), and imprint date. Lugg and Fischer's approach also includes matching titles against a large bibliographic utility's database to verify the locations and numbers of copies held elsewhere (particularly by consortial partners). The process also clearly identifies titles that should probably *not* be withdrawn, usually because a low number of copies are available elsewhere. They described the result as "an approach to deselection that is based on rules, batches, and automated support [that] enables many titles to be handled efficiently. The end result: a high-volume, high-integrity solution to moving low-use titles out of the main library—opening additional space for users" (Lugg and Fischer 2008a). One huge advantage of such a process over purely human review is that it is several orders of magnitude faster, far more accurate than the results of many librarians each applying complex criteria to the books in their own areas of expertise, and can take into account other factors, such as relative scarcity at other institutions.

Rightsizing typically involves a large (and sometime massive) initial effort to identify large quantities of material that meet the criteria for withdrawal candidates. The second stage ideally involves ongoing work to keep the collection trim and relevant for users by removing material that, over time, strays into low-use territory or becomes superseded by stable electronic access. The only reasonable way to manage such large projects is by turning to data-driven collection analysis.

There are many ways that automation helps librarians handle the daunting task of identifying titles as candidates for withdrawal, transfer to storage, or participation in consortial retention plans. For books, publication dates and circulation figures are major variables, whereas for journals, the local availability of electronic journals with perpetual access is the gold standard, although determining the relative abundance elsewhere of titles still available only in print provides another decision point. It is possible to create sophisticated queries in an integrated library system (ILS), but it is critical to be certain that the results actually represent the kinds of titles that the librarians really want to include as withdrawal candidates. "This kind of work also requires human intervention to make sure that criteria are accurate and intellectually sound, but also so that the end product bears a resemblance to what was planned" (Little 2013, 352). Computer-generated lists almost always require at least cursory review by a human being; even the most carefully crafted query cannot filter for some elements, such as flagging publications by the university president or local Nobel laureate.

The best approach to developing the criteria is to convene a team that includes the project manager and a small group of librarians representing major subject areas. At the author's institution, this group consisted of the project manager and one colleague representing science and technology and another who represented the social sciences, humanities, and business. Working with a consultant, the group developed proposed criteria that were then modified slightly by library administrators. Once established, the criteria were introduced at an Information Resources Forum to the larger group of librarians who had collection development responsibilities. Because they knew that a colleague had represented their selection area during the criteria-development process, librarians were more comfortable accepting the final criteria. It is helpful to explain that the criteria are just as much about material that will be automatically retained (e.g., books published within the past ten years and titles in special collections) as about material that will be potential withdrawal candidates. (Chapter 4 provides detailed guidance on developing withdrawal criteria for books.)

One of the virtues of integrated library systems is that experienced systems analysts can query them using multiple variables. Although circulation activity is a major factor, it no longer need be the only one. Even if the library hires a consultant to conduct the actual data analysis, the institution's librarians will make the decisions about the criteria.

Batch mode processes, although highly accurate if developed properly, are not perfect. It is inevitable that a few titles will be discarded that librarians might prefer to have kept. However, understanding that this percentage is very low, and that the collection will not be irreparably harmed by a few mistakes because almost anything can be borrowed or replaced if necessary, means that the overall benefits of batch processing over title-by-title deliberations heavily outweigh all the "what if" concerns.

If librarians from a group of libraries work to reach a common understanding on withdrawal criteria for a joint rightsizing project, some group decisions will be different from those that librarians at a single library would make. For example, librarians at an institution that scrapped its Slavic languages department ten years ago may be interested in withdrawing many of the books in that area. However, in a group endeavor for distributed holdings, they must be willing to keep some books of limited local interest to support the group's goals (e.g., maintaining at least two copies of every title held by member institutions).

MATCHING BOOKS AGAINST ELECTRONIC COLLECTIONS

Older books tend to be used less than more recently published ones. Academic libraries often have thousands of older books, frequently located in storage facilities, that not only receive very low use, but that also show significant signs of age. Many of these books were published before 1923 and thus fall into the public domain in the United States. Many of these pre-1923 titles are also relatively abundant in library collections. Many are also likely to have been digitized; some may be freely accessible at sites like Google Books and HathiTrust, or appear in collections of e-books sold by commercial vendors.

Not all patrons are completely happy with e-books, especially when reading cover-to-cover, but most would agree that e-access is a useful tool even if the print volume will be used later for close reading. Librarians' enthusiasm for e-books varies for many reasons; most have at least dabbled with buying e-books, some have wholeheartedly embraced them, and many fall somewhere in between. It is theoretically possible to weed many pre-1923 physical books and replace them with access to their electronic equivalents (Steele 2011, 160; Malpas 2011). However, the practical aspects of doing so may require time-consuming title-by-title checking. Many older bibliographic records are not as robust as current ones. Representation of the same title may vary in different systems. Some electronic collections may not have the necessary bibliographic match points of standard numbers to connect an electronic title with the physical item it duplicates. Multivolume works and monographic serials present their own headaches. Librarians raise legitimate questions about the scanning quality and completeness of digitized content on free websites. However, there is a built-in level of comfort in knowing that withdrawn print material has been replaced with the digital equivalent, even while acknowledging that a digital equivalent may not be an entirely adequate replacement.

If librarians reach the point where they agree that they can live with a certain degree of uncertainty (e.g., a few mismatches, or replacing a print copy with access to a digital copy that later proves to be unacceptable for some reason), then they can design projects to replace older content with the digital equivalents. If they buy a commercial package of older material, the vendor should provide a title list that can be matched against the collection. The lists usually require at least some title-by-title enhancements to add local call numbers, locations, and holdings, but this work can be done by staff or by student assistants. The project manager should determine in advance whether colleagues are comfortable with withdrawal activity proceeding without review by a subject specialist. If not, build a review step into the workflow.

Access issues come into play if librarians base withdrawal decisions on the availability of e-content that they have not licensed with perpetual access. If the library does not pay for the e-content and enters into a contractual relationship with the content provider, there is no guarantee that the content will be available indefinitely for the library's users. Librarians may have more confidence in the long-term viability of some of these suppliers of free e-books than of others. It is also important not to confuse e-book subscription packages with those that the library buys or licenses, because vendors of subscription products can—and do—add and subtract titles without warning.

The good news is that mass-scanning technology is continually improving. Several different organizations are involved in large projects to scan vast quantities of library collections, so the same title may be available from several sources. Some organizations allow libraries to add bibliographic records of their full-text scanned content into local catalogs or discovery layers. Not only can adding these records instantly expand discovery and access to millions of titles, but it also offers the possibility of matching them to locally held physical copies for withdrawal consideration. Librarians should not assume, however, that inclusion of a full-text work in a collection such as HathiTrust automatically means that there are sufficient print copies available to justify withdrawing local copies. Checking general availability to confirm that the titles are withdrawal candidates is still important.

An unavoidable drawback of the mass-digitization projects is that a huge percentage of the content is for material published from 1923 onward in the United States and as such is protected under copyright law (there are exceptions for some material published after this date, but identifying these titles requires special expertise). Although vast databases like HathiTrust are useful for identifying this material, patrons must still obtain and use the printed volumes or licensed electronic versions because the sites only provide bibliographic information or, at most, a snippet of the text for most material protected under copyright law.

Many publishers now offer book backlists in electronic format. Although some can be purchased on a title-by-title basis to replace print volumes, it is often more cost effective to buy backlist packages. These packages may include all or most of the publisher's titles issued before a certain date, or may be broken into subject packages. A library buying a package would not only have the option of replacing any print titles that it held, but would also acquire some new content. Other e-book collections of older titles come from vendors that have assembled packages of books from multiple publishers based on a common theme. However, it is worth considering if these older titles will actually see much use, even (or especially) in digital format. Is it worth paying to replace seldom-used titles in print with an expensive e-book package that patrons may not consult much?

As with all e-book package purchases, check the licensing agreements before purchase to confirm that the terms are satisfactory (e.g., they allow an acceptable amount of downloading and printing, permit interlibrary loan, and provide perpetual access rights).

Librarians should develop a consistent strategy for considering the withdrawal of print after acquiring e-book backfiles. It is tempting to coordinate a mass withdrawal after acquiring an e-book backfile, but remember that these titles have not been created or vetted in the same way that withdrawal lists developed in-house or by consultants usually are. For instance, it would be prudent to run a circulation report for the local print titles that match the new package, and consider retaining any print titles with significant recent circulation. Although it is possible that the availability of the electronic version will meet most of any future demand, it is also possible that patrons may prefer to consult some of the titles in print rather than electronically, especially in some disciplines. Subject librarians may also want to review the withdrawal candidates.

MATCHING JOURNALS AGAINST ELECTRONIC COLLECTIONS

Within the last decade, librarians and users alike have developed nearly complete confidence in the electronic journal as a substitute for the print one. Most academic users have successfully made the transition from feeling comfortable with the journal literature in electronic form to practically demanding it as the preferred format. Early problems with missing issues and less-than-stellar digitization have been largely resolved. Not only have librarians cancelled most print subscriptions in favor of electronic ones, but they now also feel comfortable discarding older volumes for which there are electronic equivalents with perpetual access, even when their libraries do not belong to a consortium undertaking a journal print retention effort. There is comfort in thinking of the process as exchanging one format for another—librarians are essentially removing the duplicate print versions. Note that journal withdrawal projects often proceed on a publisher-by-publisher or package-by-package basis, rather than title-by-title.

For a helpful overview of the issues surrounding the idea of withdrawing print journals when digital equivalents are available, see the report *What to Withdraw? Print Collections Management in the Wake of Digitization* (Schonfeld and Housewright 2009). Although this report was sponsored by the organization that produces JSTOR, most of the observations and recommendations are relevant for journals in general.

Electronic journals cover most of the contents of their print counterparts, but it is important to acknowledge that there is not always 100 percent equivalency. The publisher may decide not to digitize some of the print content, such as errata, advertisements, or job announcements. Other content, such as foldout maps, may be impossible to include at the time an issue is digitized. These exclusions, along with reasons such as maintaining a sufficient number of the print version, form the basis for shared print retention efforts among libraries; this topic will be explored below. On a positive note, the electronic versions sometimes include features that are absent from the print, such as links to supplementary material.

If colleagues initially mistrust the quality of digital equivalents or express concern about missing parts, it may be helpful to conduct some side-by-side comparisons such as Thomas described. After doing this, Thomas and his colleagues "found online archival publisher packages suitable for replacing print volumes," although he noted that a few titles were found not to be complete in the online version (Thomas 2011, 26). In a large rightsizing project, especially one undertaken with a looming deadline, there may not be time to check for occasional flaws or lapses in the digital product. Given that electronic titles are generally complete or nearly so, and that most images are at least adequate, librarians may have to agree that the digital product is an acceptable surrogate for the print and withdraw without taking the time for painstaking comparisons across hundreds of titles. Exceptions might be made for journals in one or two specialized disciplines, such as art or geology, that often rely on highly detailed drawings or reproductions that may not translate well to the screen. Interlibrary loan services from borrowing partners that have retained the print volumes will meet the need should patrons need a missing article.

It is important to note that libraries acquire electronic journal backfiles for two major reasons. One is to meet patron demand for immediate access to the journal literature anywhere and anytime. The other is to buy the content in this now-preferred format so that the space currently occupied by the print equivalent can be repurposed. In the process, the library often adds a significant amount of new e-content to its collection. Publishers' e-journal backfile packages usually cover titles back to the first volume, and in many cases libraries' print subscriptions began during a later year. In addition, some packages include the publishers' entire backfile (or almost all of it), not just those titles to which a particular library subscribed in print. Thus, by acquiring such a backfile, a library significantly expands the number of titles and the depth of coverage available. The author benefited from this bonus while writing this book; many library science articles that she would previously have had to request through interlibrary loan were suddenly available locally because of newly added publisher e-journal packages that contained titles to which her library had not previously subscribed. However, although a package deal may be attractive in that it adds a number of titles to which the library never subscribed, sometimes librarians feel that they pay high prices for dozens of titles that their users are unlikely to consult. If a library faces externally imposed deadlines for withdrawing large amounts of print ahead of a space repurposing project, administrators may be able to negotiate with the university for funds to purchase journal backfiles to replace print journals as part of the renovation resources arrangement.

Many libraries withdraw journal titles based on the "rule" that if they have acquired the electronic equivalent, then the print run can go. Thomas wrote that at his library "we have made the decision that the online format is a true substitution and we should treat it as such by removing print volumes whenever feasible" (Thomas 2011, 26).

Titles for which publishers or certain aggregators offer electronic backfiles and subscriptions usually offer a high level of security. Organizations such as Portico, LOCKSS (Lots of Copies Keep Stuff Safe), and CLOCKSS (Controlled LOCKSS) have missions to maintain publisher-submitted journal files so that should a publisher fail, libraries that previously paid for perpetual access rights to that content can continue to access it per their licensing agreements. Both publishers and libraries can join these organizations as participating members to sustain this important function of long-term archiving of digital content. Librarians whose libraries have bought perpetual access to journal backfiles can feel confident withdrawing the print equivalent, although there may be reasons to retain selected titles in print even with electronic access. It is helpful to establish a workflow for processing each publisher's journal list as the library buys backfiles. For details on the operational aspects of withdrawing print journals, see chapter 4.

Librarians can safely decide to withdraw print journals with electronic equivalents without worrying that they might be discarding scarce print copies. The very availability of the electronic versions confirms that print copies are widely available, because publishers and vendors only go to the expense of producing electronic backfiles in cases where there are many potential buyers. Besides the archived electronic versions at organizations like Portico, a growing number of consortia have undertaken to collect and maintain complete print runs of journal titles with electronic equivalents. Consortially maintained print runs may be recorded centrally at sites like the Print Archive and Preservation Registry (PAPR), although librarians should be aware that the managers of some consortial journal projects may not contribute holdings in a timely manner, or indeed may not do so at all. Still, there is now a large enough mass of titles listed in PAPR that a library could make at least some withdrawal decisions based on the listings there, secure in the knowledge that enough geographically dispersed libraries have made commitments to hold the print and to supply occasional articles or volumes through interlibrary loan.

Withdrawing journal titles that have electronic equivalents is the obvious first choice because the library is simply replacing content in one format (print) with the same content in another format (digitial). Most patrons have already happily abandoned the periodical stacks for online access. Multiple backup options exist (both electronic and print), and withdrawing what now amounts to print duplicates frees up literally miles of shelf space.

WITHDRAWALS BASED ON SHORT RUNS OR SCATTERED HOLDINGS

The approach of withdrawing incomplete titles is one that works for both books and journals. If a library holds only a few volumes of older multivolume sets, and if they show no or low circulation, librarians might decide to withdraw them if they are not scarce titles. However, identifying these relatively few orphans in a large book collection may be difficult.

It is easier to take this approach with journals, but librarians face different challenges if they decide to withdraw old or partial print runs of journal titles for which there is as yet no electronic equivalent or for which pre-1923 electronic holdings are included in a digitization project (quality varies and perpetual access may not be assured). Typically, this project might be the next step after working with journals that have electronic equivalents.

Librarians must develop these lists themselves, usually based on an ILS query to identify print serial titles and local holdings. Then it is relatively easy to review the list and identify those titles with short runs or scattered holdings, bearing in mind that a run such as v.6(1963)–v.10(1967) may indicate a short period of a title change in a long-running title. It is also important to check bibliographic utilities' database holdings information to determine which other libraries have the title, remembering that holdings information is not always present or, if present, may not always be accurate. It may be necessary to check selected libraries' catalogs, perhaps those of consortial members with large collections, to determine actual holdings. These are time-consuming but necessary steps because librarians do not inadvertently want to discard even scattered issues of an older journal with only a few other holding libraries in the country. Still, considerable shelf space can be recovered by removing a large number of journal runs with short or scattered holdings. For a description of one library's method for handling such a project, which took into account factors such as language and holdings at selected consortial partners, see Ward and Aagard's article (Ward and Aagard 2008).

DIGITIZATION

One difficult aspect of many rightsizing projects is that reviewing the book collection means identifying many titles as withdrawal candidates that, unlike journals, have no electronic equivalent. One inevitable question arises: "Can't we just digitize the material before we discard the print volumes so that the content will still be available for our users?"

Many academic libraries offer digitization services. They often digitize material in their archives and special collections. Material published by their own institutions, such as technical reports, alumni newsletters, administrative documents, and agricultural bulletins, are obvious candidates for local digitization. Crumbling nineteenth-century books may be candidates because they are no longer protected by copyright laws and are often too fragile for routine circulation; these efforts may focus as much on preservation as on access.

However, libraries face many challenges related to digitization: legal, financial, and practical. The challenges and opportunities of managing library digitization services deserve book-length coverage, but here is a short summary of major aspects as they relate to rightsizing.

Legally, libraries cannot scan and post copyright-protected material (generally items issued from 1923 onwards in the United States) without the copyright holder's permission. Identifying copyright holders or identifying post-1922 works that might be in the public domain can be a long and difficult process. The copyright holder is not always the author; it may be the publisher (which may now be out of business or have been absorbed by another company) or it could be the author's heirs. Efforts are being made to identify "orphan" works for which it proves impossible, after diligent effort, to identify the rightsholder. If the rightsholders give their written permission, with or without requesting the payment of a fee, then libraries or commercial ventures can digitize these titles. People who trace rightsholders of decades-old works are usually convinced that the value of the work is sufficiently high to warrant the amount of time and other costs involved in the tracking process; relatively few works fall into this category.

Financially, establishing, managing, and operating a digitization service is very expensive in terms of space, staff, and equipment. Equipment costs go beyond the initial price; there are supplies, warranties or service contracts, insurance, and eventually replacement costs to consider. Staffing costs far more than hiring a dozen student assistants to conduct the scanning procedure. Full-time staff manage the operation, and usually a group of librarians is tasked with identifying titles and collections to scan, writing grant proposals to fund large projects, prioritizing tasks, training and supervising staff, preparing manuals to ensure professional-level scanning, and making decisions about how to organize and upload the resulting scans and metadata using specialized software. Although there may be a fee-based component to accommodate some requests for digitizing specific items, this is often a small percentage of the total budget. The library must pay for the whole operation, usually from a combination of the annual budget and grant funds. Sustainability is a constant concern. The annual output may be relatively modest with many proposals in the project queue. The managers usually seek projects that reflect the institution's prestige or that have a relatively high likelihood for use by both the local and wider population.

Practically, even if the legal copyright issues can be solved at a reasonable expense, few library-based digitization services can afford to scan dozens, much less hundreds or thousands, of obscure out-of-print titles that were seldom or never used recently in their print manifestations. Such large-scale scanning projects have been undertaken by very large research libraries (often with a focus on a specific collection or type of material), by commercial firms that then charge libraries to buy the resulting digitized collections, by extremely large companies that seem to have endlessly deep pockets, or by coalitions of research libraries pooling resources. Unlike the large-scale commercial digitization of material like journals, small-scale local digitization is not generally intended as a solution to replace older material *en masse,* but rather to meet some combination of preservation and access needs for specific titles with particular relevance to the local institution. In these cases, the library does not discard the original document after digitization, but rather retains it as a historical or cultural artifact.

For most individual libraries, it is not economically feasible to scan large quantities of no-use or low-use material with the sole aim of replacing withdrawn print resources with their digital equivalents. Keep in mind that many out-of-copyright titles may have already been scanned by one or more of the mega-projects, and may thus already be freely available on the Internet. However, delaying withdrawals until the digital equivalents are available may not be a sound practice. If the rightsizing criteria have been developed properly, the withdrawal candidates are all readily available through interlibrary loan for those rare occasions when a patron may require them in the future. Librarians can remove the titles eligible for withdrawal, secure in the knowledge that even if there is no digital equivalent available, the resource-sharing safety net assures rapid access.

COLLABORATIVE STORAGE

A library can certainly undertake a rightsizing project on its own. However, there are further potential benefits from coordinating at least part of a rightsizing effort with those of other libraries. Many libraries with similar or complementary collections in a region or consortium will be in some stage of contemplating their own plans to reduce the size of their physical collections.

It makes sense to explore ways in which some of this work could be done collaboratively. Sooner or later, managers of libraries with rapidly filling primary location shelves or remote storage facilities "become increasingly eager to find a more sustainable approach to print storage, which has in turn led to growing interest in the advantages offered by collaborative or shared print repositories" (Genoni 2012, 24).

Even the most ardent rightsizing advocate is keenly aware of the broader need to keep adequate back-up print copies. Although it is true that not every academic library needs to keep every print title it ever acquired, it is also true that as a profession we need to make consistent, concerted efforts to retain a reasonable number of geographically dispersed copies. One logical and cost-efficient way to do this is at the consortial level, working with trusted partners who already collaborate in areas such as resource sharing, collection development, and electronic licensing.

Why collaborate? People learned millennia ago that a group can accomplish far more than an individual and, theoretically at least, each individual in the group expends less effort for more reward when acting cooperatively. Libraries attract employees who have positive service attitudes and who are predisposed towards collaborative solutions. Librarians are trained to help others and to cooperate to achieve service objectives of mutual benefit to all participants. The concept of resource sharing, for example, is hardwired into librarians' service philosophy. What other profession would on a daily basis send thousands of items purchased with local funds to colleagues all over the country for the use of those colleagues' customers, all at either no direct cost at all, or for at most a cost-recovery fee?

There are two major collaborative storage options: joint storage facilities and distributed retention plans.

Some consortia or geographically close libraries have participated for decades in joint storage facilities or other joint print retention arrangements. Others are only just beginning to consider the advantages of taking group action to make retention decisions. Joint storage facilities come in several different flavors. In Ohio, five regional book repositories serve academic libraries throughout the state. In California, two regional facilities serve the ten campuses of the University of California. In Denver, one storage facility serves several area libraries. The Research Collections and Preservation Consortium (ReCAP), located in New Jersey, is a joint endeavor between Columbia University, the New York Public Library, and Princeton University. Indiana University's Auxiliary Library Facility (ALF) holds the Shared Print Repository of the Committee on Institutional Cooperation (CIC), in addition to holding certain local library material in storage. These are just some of many joint endeavors.

The second kind of collaborative print retention is the distributed model. Member libraries contribute their holdings information (with circulation data for books) to a central authority or consultant who analyzes the data. The end result of this complex analysis is a number of action lists. Each library receives a list of no- and low-use books which it can now discard because sufficient copies (usually two or three) are held elsewhere in the group and those holding libraries have agreed to maintain those copies for the good of the group. Each library also receives a list of the books that it must maintain locally so that others may discard their low-use copies. This model works in a similar fashion for journals: each library agrees to hold certain titles in print so that other libraries in the group may discard their print runs. These are usually journals for which full electronic coverage exists and to which the member libraries also have access, often through a consortial license. When a library commits to retaining certain titles as part of a distributed retention model, staff usually add notes or codes to certain fields in the corresponding bibliographic records so that that this material is not inadvertently weeded in later local rightsizing activities.

The notion of large storage facilities operated on a collaborative basis is not new. In 1950, Rogers wrote that

> the regional depository library provides the means for cooperative stor-
> age of little-used materials of research significance, such storage being
> predicated upon economy of cost and service to participating libraries.
> This, perhaps is a fair statement of the short-term purposes of regional
> depository centers. It is quite possible that long-term realities may con-
> siderably extend these original functions. (Rogers 1950, 147).

Rogers recognized that founding and maintaining such facilities would be very expensive, perhaps even too expensive for the participating libraries to bear all the costs. He suggested involving the federal government in funding a series of regional depository libraries, although this plan never materialized (Rogers 1950, 149). Colwell admonished academic libraries, even research libraries, that they "should not try to contain the reserves for the future, nor . . . perpetuate the catastrophes of the past." Scholars and librarians should not "live like academic squirrels" by trying to envision a future that they cannot possibly predict. He recommended that the regional library "develop the research library resources of the entire region" held for "our common use" (Colwell 1949, 196–98).

As librarians reach the conclusion that each of their individual institutions cannot possibly sustain the acquisition, maintenance, digitization, and preservation needs of collections that in large part duplicate those of other institutions, collaborative efforts offer many advantages, not least of which is the ability to withdraw large amounts of no- and low-use print secure in the knowledge that partners are maintaining sufficient copies should they be needed. Each library also contributes or agrees to keep certain no- and low-use print titles as part of its participation in the larger effort to maintain sufficient copies within the research community. Collaborating on print reten-tion projects ultimately represents cost savings for each individual library, but it also represents the investment of both time and money by the members as a whole.

A collaborative print retention plan requires several elements. Strong leadership is essential. The group may already work together as a consortium, in which case the trust, cooperative mechanisms, and at least some level of organizational structure are already in place. In other instances, the group may be a new combination of cooperating partners that has just embarked on working with colleagues who are less well-known. In either case, it is essential to establish a governing structure and a few small working groups to develop agreements to guide the consortium's efforts. A memorandum of agreement (MOU) outlines each member's responsibilities and commitments.

The group that governs the effort usually consists of members at the high-est level, such as library directors. The governing group approves and oversees membership fees, coordinates system development, approves policies pro-posed by any working groups, and advises on the project's overall direction.

Developing the group's goals is an essential early step. As an example, here are the goals for the Committee on Institutional Cooperation's (CIC) Shared Print Repository (www.cic.net/projects/library/shared-print-repository/goals):

1. Aggregate, secure, and preserve the rich print resources developed by CIC libraries over the past two centuries.
2. Ensure that CIC scholars and students have timely access to these archived resources.
3. Realize the economies of scale made possible through collective action that will allow CIC libraries to apply best practices for storing, preserv-ing, servicing, and reflecting print holdings well into the future.
4. Help CIC campuses reclaim local resources, including space, funds, and staff time by relieving them of the obligation to store lesser-used redundant material.
5. Integrate CIC libraries into an emerging national network of collec-tively managed research library resources.

The CIC is a group of research libraries located mainly in the Midwest. The CIC's Center for Library Initiatives' (CLI) first goal is to gather complete jour-nal runs from major publishers into a high-density storage facility owned and maintained by one of the members. Three of its working groups have:

- developed standards, policies, and best practices for activities such as compiling lists of material to be gathered and stored;
- determined standards for bibliographic records;
- decided how closely to check incoming material for completeness and validation;

- determined minimum acceptable conditions of incoming material;
- decided which members will contribute which titles;
- set terms and conditions for lending to members and non-members; and
- created policies for action in the case of volumes lost or damaged while borrowed.

CIC member libraries are also interested in exploring the possibility of some kind of cooperative print management for books. Along with many other academic libraries, CIC library administrators understand that "shared print archiving offers a strategic solution for collective action to assure preservation of sufficient print copies nationally as collections are drawn down locally" (Demas and Lougee 2011, 1). In 2014, OCLC issued *Right-scaling Stewardship: A Multi-scale Perspective on Cooperative Print Management,* a report that looked at the issue both from the perspective of one of the member libraries and from the perspective of the entire consortium (Malpas and Lavoie 2014). This report's major findings include the following:

- Shared print strategies not only focus on reducing redundancy among member libraries, but also identify both local and group strengths.
- There is future opportunity for library consortia to expand their print management activities to include other regional libraries that are not consortial members.
- "Uniqueness is rare, but rareness is common."
- The print book collection at one library, The Ohio State University (OSU), duplicated the other consortial members' collection, ranging between 31 and 59 percent.
- The percentage of OSU's print book collection that was duplicated in other members' collections ranged between 20 and 49 percent.
- The percentage of OSU's print book collection held by at least one other consortial member ranged between 93 and 76 percent, or overall 83 percent of OSU's collection was held by at least one other member.
- Each local collection has a significant rare element of titles that are not widely held by other consortial partners.
- Consortial members are highly interconnected with thousands of other libraries worldwide through interlibrary loan services (both borrowing and lending).
- Interlibrary loan traffic suggests that other non-consortial regional libraries benefit from the resources available in CIC libraries.
- Shared print strategies reduce costs and can enhance access to collective print resources for all the members' constituents.

The report concluded that "managing, providing access to, and preserving the collective print book resource must be a shared responsibility, because no single institutional collection (or even group-scale resource) has a reasonable approximation of the complete corpus of material, either overall or in any particular subject area" (Malpas and Lavoie 2014, 46).

It is important to realize that no library can commit to holding something *forever*. If the expected time commitment stretches more than about twenty-five years into the future, the officers expected to sign the group agreement may become less happy about doing so. Although it may be likely that if a library agrees to keep a journal run for twenty-five years it will probably also be able to hold it for fifty, no one likes to make the longer commitment at the outset. So many social, economic, national, local, political, environmental, preservation, technological, publishing, educational, and other conditions may change radically over even a few decades. The governing group should set a realistic future retention date to which members feel comfort committing, and then review it for an extension when the expiration date approaches.

One question that arises early in joint storage arrangements is who owns the item? Is it the library that sent the piece to the facility, or is it the library that houses it? Or, is there some kind of joint ownership managed by the consortium or other institutional body? The question of ownership is an important one for several reasons. In some states, the rules for disposition of property acquired by state-supported institutions are very specific. Although the outright disposal of unwanted property may be possible according to state regulations, can the library send print journal runs to a partner's facility in the next state? If the storage facility in the next-door state agrees to house the volumes but not claim ownership of them, the transfer may be possible.

Some joint facilities allow each member to deposit whatever they wish and to maintain ownership of those titles. Although this approach solves some of the potential difficulties of managing a joint facility, it also means that there will inevitably be some duplication of holdings, because more than one library may deposit the same titles. As the facility fills up, members may discuss deduplication; this task will be harder to manage after deposit. Having a clause in the agreements that prohibits the deposit of duplicate titles should solve this problem, as long as all members have access to all titles, whether they were the depositing library or not.

It is easy to underestimate the amount of time needed to handle a consortial journal print retention project. Simply gathering the serial holdings information from each member is a major challenge. Many different ILS vendors will be involved. The staff at each institution have differing technical abilities to produce the required lists. Once obtained, the lists need to be merged and holdings compared. Which libraries have the longest runs of each title? What is the best way to handle dozens of cases in which a complete run must be assembled from the partial holdings of several libraries? How should title changes be accommodated? Sometimes titles do not simply change: they explode into multiple parts. Who determines if pieces meet minimum condition standards? Who checks for completeness? What happens when a title that was sent as a complete run turns out to have missing volumes? Who pays for shipping volumes to the facility that will house them? How should the housing library's holdings reflect titles that become part of the consortium's joint serial collection? The answers to these questions will be codified in the consortium's joint retention program agreement.

A final important piece is maintaining an up-to-date list of titles that have been added to the shared repository, along with standard information such as holdings, publisher's name, and ISSN. Decide whether to list titles for which only partial holdings have been obtained, or whether to wait until the whole run is present before adding a title. If partial holdings appear on the list, mark them in some way to indicate this. It is also extremely helpful to add the date on which a title entered the list. Member libraries using the list to draw down their local print holdings will consult this list periodically, and staff will want an easy way to filter out titles that they have already checked.

It is also useful for a print retention cooperative to collaborate with similar efforts when feasible. Listing the consortium's holdings with the Print Archives Preservation Registry (PAPR) is a step in this direction. Libraries that are not part of these consortia may use PAPR's lists to inform their own print journal retention decisions. In the longer term, there may be opportunities to rightsize consortial holdings. There are many examples of duplicate print journal runs across the consortia that list their holdings in PAPR. At some point in the future, when users and librarians feel even more comfortable with electronic journal coverage and backup options, the number of print runs for some of these titles could be reduced further, paying attention to geographic distribution. See figure 3.1 for an example of journal titles with consortial holdings from the PAPR list.

Although journals are usually the starting point for a group of libraries beginning a collaborative venture, identifying low-use books represents another opportunity for maintaining a few copies within a consortium and allowing other members to discard theirs. Although the retention copies may be housed centrally, the distributed model is currently a popular option. Libraries tag their catalog records to flag titles that are part of their commitment to keep certain works.

American academic libraries are moving away from the twentieth-century trend of simply warehousing low-use material locally to the encouraging twenty-first–century trend of "collaborating on who, how, and what to store [so that] libraries can start the process of strategically drawing down their print collections while still maintaining access" (Clement 2012, 164). A summary of a 2003 conference reported that attendees agreed that management of print resources would be optimized "when it provides the scholarly community the

FIGURE 3.1.

Examples of Journal Title Entries from the Print
Archives Preservation Registry (PAPR)

Title	Publisher	ISSN	Program (Institution)
IEEE transactions on haptics	IEEE	1939-1412	WEST (ZAPSP) UCL Shared Print (ZAPSP)
IEEE transactions on human factors in electronics	Institute of Electrical and Electronics Engineers	0096-249X	WEST (ZAPSP) UCL Shared Print (ZAPSP) PORTICO COPPUL SPAN (CONCUF) LHL (LHL) ASERL (GAT)
IEEE transactions on image processing/a publication of the IEEE Signal Processing Society	Institute of Electrical and Electronics Engineers	1057-7149	WEST (ZAPSP) UCL Shared Print (ZAPSP) PORTICO LHL (LHL) ASERL (GAT)
IEEE transactions on industrial electronics: a publication of the IEEE Industrial Electronics Society	Institute of Electrical and Electronics Engineers	0278-0046	WEST (ZAPSP) UCL Shared Print (ZAPSP) PORTICO COPPUL SPAN (CONCUF) ASERL (GAT)
IEEE transactions on industrial electronics and control instrumentation	Professional Technical Group on Industrial Electronics and Control Instrumentation	0018-9421	WEST (ZAPSP) UCL Shared Print (ZAPSP) PORTICO COPPUL SPAN (CONCUF) LHL (LHL) ASERL (GAT)
IEEE transactions on industrials electronics	Professional Technical Group on Industrial Electronics	0099-4553	WEST (ZAPSP) UCL Shared Print (ZAPSP) LHL (LHL) ASERL (GAT)

SOURCE: papr.crl.edu

greatest possible richness and diversity of knowledge resources, minimizes
inadvertent loss, and makes the most efficient use of available human and
financial resources. Inexpensive storage was considered to be only a partial
solution, in itself of little value unless combined with rigorous and active
management of materials and metadata" (Reilly 2005, 103).

For journals especially, the question arises of how carefully should the
staff at the institution holding the volumes check to see that they are complete? Part of the answer lies in the rationale for assembling complete runs
of selected titles. Is preservation (dark archive) the reason, or is the organization gathering "service" copies as circulating backup volumes should someone need one (light archive)? Several groups strive for page-level verification
in the interests of preserving runs, whereas others are satisfied with the less
time-consuming issue-level or volume-level verification, balancing the ability

to acquire and store large numbers of titles fairly quickly against the knowl-edge that a few pages, articles, or even issues will be missing. Knowing that there are both a few page-verified preservation runs as well as numerous ser-vice runs held in various print retention repositories, as well as digital copies deposited with organizations like Portico, librarians can feel confident with-drawing their local volumes of these titles. Their licensed access to the elec-tronic versions will meet almost all patron demand, but there are multiple print backup copies available should the need arise.

How many archived print copies in one country or on one continent are sufficient? Nobody has the definitive answer. Librarians would agree that for books, fifty copies are probably too many and five are probably too few. Not all archive facilities are the same; for example, some are climate controlled, and others are not, so print volumes in some locations may still be in good usable condition several hundred years from now, whereas others may not be. Over time, some losses and deterioration are inevitable for the great masses of vol-umes in high-density storage. Over long periods of time, distributed archiving in open stacks circulating collections is not as reliable as centralized archiving in a closed storage facility. Geographical dispersion means that any partic-ular library is probably within a few hundred miles of a facility able to sup-ply a non-scarce title. Copies in multiple locations mean that should one, or even several facilities, experience calamities such as fire, flood, earthquake, or mold, there will still be several print duplicates of most titles elsewhere. None of these arrangements will be foolproof forever, but our profession has made excellent progress on the task of ensuring that multiple copies of most printed works will be maintained in sufficient numbers for the foreseeable future.

COST

Everyone naturally wants to know about costs. Rightsizing sounds expensive. There are staffing costs, and deploying current employees means that these people will not be available to do some of their other work during the proj-ect. Hiring a consultant for part of the process is not a common expense in the annual budget. There will be some costs associated with moving material out, buying extra boxes or containers or book carts, paying additional recy-cling fees, and campus publicity. Collaborative print retention may be less expensive in the long run, but there are costs associated with these activi-ties. Studies, articles, and reports exist or can be compiled to show annual cost-per-retained-volume in several different kinds of library locations, or the typical cost per square foot of new library construction. Lee's comprehensive article, "The Library Space Problem, Future Demand, and Collection Control," explored various methods of calculating costs; in its section about weeding costs this sentence stands out: "Researchers disagree on how to calculate these specific costs" (Lee 1993, 155). Martin and Manch also noted "that the costs vary considerably from one report to another and that meaningful weeding costs may be difficult to determine. Any report describing the 'high' cost of weeding should consider seriously the 'higher' cost of retention and preservation" (Martin and Manch 1971, 600).

It is natural for administrators to ponder at least some of the following points. Would it be cheaper in the long run to build a storage facility, or to expand the library or an existing storage facility, and just keep all the low-use physical library material? If the library is not quite full yet, perhaps we could defer making retention decisions for a few more years and save project costs now. Would it be sufficient just to weed selected areas of the collection a little bit at a time over the next few years? What if we only withdraw journal volumes for which we have perpetual electronic access? Should we wait until our library consortium has firmed up collaborative storage plans?

There may be good reasons to delay, but many libraries have arrived at a point where they cannot wait much longer; some solution must be found, and found quickly, because either the stacks are practically bursting or some external event has forced the issue. Even if a solution does not have to begin immediately, administrators realize that ultimately it is not a helpful strategy to delay action for a few years until the situation does become critical. A solution that is expensive today will become even more so five years from now.

This book will not try to provide cost information. Costs vary widely depending on many factors, including the availability of space in an already-constructed storage facility and its distance from the campus libraries; the number of library locations on a particular campus, local staff salaries, local costs for hiring temporary workers or student employees, total collection size and amount of material that will eventually be withdrawn, and local recycling or other disposal options. Costs also depend on whether or not some fairly recent weeding activities have already taken place; whether the library hires a consultant and, if so, what work the consultant undertakes; whether or not librarians review all, some, or none of the withdrawal candidate lists; and whether the library is an active participant in a consortial collaborative storage project.

It is important to realize that there are also costs associated with *not* undertaking a rightsizing project when it is clear that one would bring much-needed relief. Some of these costs are measurable, such as the staff costs of trying to shelve in tightly packed areas and constantly shifting material to try to make room for new arrivals. Others are intangible, such as the increased level of user frustration that comes with jam-packed shelves, the higher likelihood of mis-shelved material, and the diminished ability to find relevant items among all the obsolete ones. It is worth noting that the costs of not rightsizing are ongoing, whereas once most items have traveled the path from no- or low-use shelf-sitter through disposal, there are no further tangible costs associated with them (the exceptions being infrequent interlibrary loan or repurchase costs).

Costs also change over time, and not just with inflation. Technological advances have made compiling and managing withdrawal candidate lists much easier and faster than they were even ten years ago; it is likely that they will be even easier (and possibly cheaper) ten years from now (although this is not a reason to defer a rightsizing project!).

The cost of a rightsizing project can also be regarded at least in part as previous costs deferred. Had routine reviews taken place in the past, the current situation would be far less dire. Although this is now water under the bridge, this fact should help underscore the benefits of continuing regular reviews of the physical collection after the initial rightsizing project has been completed.

4

Project Management

A S WE HAVE SEEN, A LIBRARY MAY START ITS RIGHTSIZING
activities in any one of several different ways: going solo with its own book
collection, beginning to withdraw print journal titles after licensing perpetual
access to the same content in e-journal format, becoming an active member
of a joint storage facility, or joining a group of regional libraries implementing a distributed print retention plan of either books or journals. Of course,
a library's rightsizing plan may be motivated by some combination of these
activities.

Whatever the reason for a library's involvement in rightsizing, a key factor in successful project management is the assignment of an effective project manager and sufficient resources to complete the work within the desired
time frame.

Small or routine weeding projects, such as reviewing the reference collection over the summer, can be carried out using existing staff as part of their
regular duties as can the routine annual or biennial activities that follow a
massive retroactive rightsizing project. However, the initial retroactive rightsizing project is a larger endeavor that often involves multiple locations and
multiple formats. It may be driven by tight deadlines and it may continue for

several years. It includes significant physical movement of material—to local storage facilities, to joint storage facilities, to used book vendors, to recycling, or frequently to multiple destinations. Shifting remaining material may be necessary, and if one project goal is repurposing space, then stacks shelving may need to be moved—or removed—afterwards. Recordkeeping involves tracking tens or hundreds of thousands of titles and volumes through identification, review, removal, and catalog updates. Rightsizing projects require a project manager: someone who plans the work, oversees forward momentum, keeps track of all the moving parts, troubleshoots any difficulties, and keeps the administration informed. The manager need not take on the project as his or her sole responsibility, but a significant portion of his or her time should be freed to focus on the work. Library administrators should clearly indicate their support of the project and emphasize that the manager has the authority to act on their behalf in coordinating and directing the work of other employees who may not normally report to him or her.

Besides appointing the right person as manager, staffing the project properly is also crucial to its success. Some rightsizing projects may work well with the manager coordinating staff and resources as needed. In other libraries, the manager leads a designated project team. Some team members may be wholly or partially reassigned to work on various aspects of the rightsizing project. Some libraries hire temporary workers or additional student assistants to handle tasks like removing volumes from the shelves or packing them for delivery to a used book dealer. A full- or part-time special projects librarian who handles or coordinates list generation as well as journal location and holdings lookups can be an extremely helpful addition to the effort.

The initial effort of rightsizing the physical collection may be one of the largest projects that a library ever undertakes. It is not realistic to expect a miraculous and accurate completion of the project with only a few people working on it as time permits. In some situations, the rightsizing project will take many years before it reaches the routine maintenance stage. In others, a relatively short deadline may drive rapid completion of at least some of the work.

STRATEGIC RIGHTSIZING APPROACH

Most academic libraries have evaluated their collections (or at least parts of them) over time, but often these reviews have been piecemeal, relying on the interest and efforts of specific librarians in particular locations, driven by crowding in one section of the stacks, or inspired by the availability of new storage space (in which case librarians often just transfer low-use material rather than making decisions about withdrawal and retention).

More recently, librarians have begun withdrawing print serials when they have been replaced by electronic equivalents, but even this activity sometimes takes place in some locations but not in others. The ability to compare one's own monograph collection against those of peer institutions now allows libraries to consider mass withdrawals based both on low use locally and wide availability elsewhere. Now is the time for library administrators to consider the many changing factors in the academic environment and to make a long-term strategic commitment to rightsize the physical collection.

The previous chapter on new solutions introduced the idea of the rightsizing plan and outlined its essential elements. By the time the administration starts implementing the project, the withdrawal policy and the rightsizing plan should be written and approved. The project manager should be appointed and, if a team approach is preferred, the team put in place. The manager's first job is to develop an action plan and time line. What part of the project should be tackled first? Is there a logical way to start with a small pilot to test procedures? If there are deadlines, what are they? Do deadlines apply to the whole project, or only to parts of it? If both books and journals are on the to-do list, what is the best way to organize the work if they have to be handled simultaneously instead of sequentially? Who can help with various tasks? Are there any opportunities to work collaboratively with other libraries on any part of the project? Is it feasible to hire a consultant to help develop book withdrawal candidate lists? Are there any special supplies or equipment that will be needed? How much of the work can be achieved using existing staff? Is hiring temporary staff for specific tasks feasible? How can the tasks be broken into manageable pieces? What is the best way to track progress on all subdivided parts so that nothing falls through the cracks? The following sections discuss managing the rightsizing project in a way that addresses these questions.

DISPOSAL OF WITHDRAWN MATERIAL

Disposing of withdrawn material is typically the last step in the rightsizing workflow, so why is it important to consider it very early in the planning process? There are many potential options for the withdrawn items' ultimate destination, but usually only a few viable alternatives for each library, based on a combination of many factors including local regulations, the available space in staging areas, the speed with which the project must be carried out, or funds available for paying for the preferred (or required) method of disposal. Reaching an understanding very early about what will ultimately happen to the withdrawn material means that the manager avoids the possibility of ramping up a rightsizing project and then discovering that work must be suspended to finalize disposal arrangements that, depending on the method chosen, may be unexpectedly time consuming.

What university regulations or, if applicable, state laws govern the disposal of library material? Are there general guidelines for disposal of university-purchased items, perhaps dependent on their value or initial cost? Does a state-funded institution need to follow certain laws regarding the disposal of state property? If these guidelines, regulations, or laws are restrictive, out-dated, unclear, or otherwise difficult to follow, can the library apply for an exception? In one state where selling state property was prohibited, librarians gave away unwanted material by placing it on a book cart near the front door, but it is important to think through possible negative reactions from stake-holders before taking this approach with a large quantity of library discards rather than with a few unwanted gifts (Handis 2007, 85).

Here are some possible options for disposing of withdrawn material.

Book Sales

Many academic libraries have periodic public sales of withdrawn books and unwanted gifts. The advantage is that the library raises some money. Disad-vantages include the considerable amount of time required to set up and staff the sale; storage space for material designated for the sale; the necessity of stamping all items as library discards; effort needed to sort books into subject categories and to price them; university rules for accepting payments; possi-ble restrictions on how the raised funds can be used; and the need to store or dispose of unsold books. Will someone sort out obvious items that no one will buy, such as outdated test preparation manuals and old supplements to busi-ness reference books? Potential buyers are usually only interested in books, not in material in other formats. In addition, a rightsizing project may gen-erate tens of thousands of withdrawn books within a fairly short time span, and handling a book sale on this scale may be beyond the scope of the typical annual event.

Bookstore

Some libraries have small resale shops where they sell selected unwanted donations or withdrawn books. Will the store be able to accommodate the flood of withdrawn books from a rightsizing project, including many that have very little potential for a possible sale? If not, is it worth the time to cull through thousands of outdated books to identify the few that might attract interest in the shop? Where will the library store books as they wait to move into the limited bookstore space?

Auction

Book resellers may be interested in buying books in lots, sight unseen. A library might try attracting bidders for "300 boxes of assorted books." This option involves stamping each volume to show that it has been officially withdrawn;

advertising the auction; managing the bids; being sure that the payment clears the bank before releasing the goods; scheduling a mutually acceptable time for the high bidder to pick up the boxes; determining potential liability issues if library staff help with moving or loading boxes; and possibly dealing with disgruntled unsuccessful bidders, or even a disgruntled buyer who feels, upon examination, that most of the "assorted books" have very little resale value. (To avoid the last situation, the library should also make it clear at the outset that the books are not returnable.)

Selling Selected Titles Online

Public libraries have had some success selling selected titles through online bookselling and auction venues. This avenue requires time to identify potential withdrawn books to sell; space for processing, holding, and packing books; researching prices; providing equipment; a commitment to handling sales and customer queries in a timely manner; sturdy packaging materials; possible trips to the post office to avoid mixing sale books with regular outgoing library mail; accounting responsibilities; and so forth. Academic libraries may find that implementing this solution using regular staff may be more difficult given various university accounting guidelines and other regulations. Public libraries often solve this staffing dilemma by assigning volunteers from the institution's Friends of the Library group, but this option may not be available for academic libraries.

Salvage

Many institutions hold periodic sales of surplus property (e.g., furniture, computers, and other tangible assets). One library that sent withdrawn material to be included in one such sale found that very few items were sold (Metz and Gray 2005, 276).

Offering Titles to Other Institutions

Years ago, staff in library gift-and-exchange units circulated lists of unwanted items in the hope that other libraries might buy some of them. Because so many libraries are now involved in rightsizing activities, there will be few takers for withdrawn items. One library required by state law to offer weeded titles to other state institutions found, not surprisingly, that there were no takers for their unwanted journal volumes (Tobia 2002, 98). Another library sent its journal discard list to other academic libraries in the state and ultimately sent three other libraries a total of 236 volumes (out of nearly 11,000) (Gallagher and Rathemacher 2012, 99). Yet another library had some luck posting book discard lists to a statewide listserv and then using the state's library courier service to send some titles to other institutions that had asked for them (Fohl 2001, 49). One library selected some discards from the English and American literature section to send to an in-state correctional facility (Metz and Gray 2005, 275). A library discarding JSTOR volumes may wish to check with one of several sites that collect complete JSTOR runs; these facilities often post wish lists of volumes that they lack. (Check in advance before mailing any volumes on the list.) The author has contacted colleagues at other libraries and successfully donated small runs of miscellaneous older theses to those institutions and, in several cases, has arranged to send volumes of nineteenth-century periodicals to the Center for Research Libraries to fill gaps in their holdings.

Recycling

This may be the best option for some material, particularly bound journal volumes, which have almost no resale value. The library should work closely with the campus recycling office, especially when handling the massive amounts of material generated from multiple locations by a rightsizing project over several months or years. It is critical to arrange a secure hand-off from library locations to recycling personnel. More than one library has found itself plunged into a maelstrom of negative publicity after a curious passerby rummaged through a container left open and unattended on a loading dock. It may also be possible to recycle microform in a separate stream. Some libraries shred withdrawn print material.

Donation to Third World Countries

Someone will inevitably suggest donating the discarded material to universities overseas. Quite apart from the shipping costs of such a venture (who pays?), it would be of dubious value (if not ethically questionable) to donate outdated books on bridge building, nursing, medicine, agriculture, and many other subjects. Still, if the institution has a special relationship with a university overseas that might be interested in some of the library's discards, it may be worth pursuing this option.

Giving Material Away

One library made it possible for faculty to "select books that they wish to add to their private collections," a practice that might not only be impractical at a large institution, but that might also raise legal issues at a state-supported institution (Soma and Sjoberg 2011, 24). At other libraries, patrons could help themselves to discarded books left on a cart in the lobby (Handis 2007, 85; Dubicki 2008, 134).

Working with a Single Large Book Reseller

The library may decide to work with a major commercial book reseller to dispose of virtually all its discarded books (journals are usually of no interest). The reseller typically offers a contract to pay a certain (low) price per book, with an additional payment should selected individual books sell above a predetermined price. The library should ask the university contracts office to review and approve such an arrangement well in advance of implementation. Choosing this option may lead to situations in which other book dealers express dissatisfaction that there is now no longer an avenue for them to have a chance to buy or bid on the books.

Choosing the Best Options

Because there are many options, it makes sense to settle on the one or two that make the most sense for the local situation and for the types and quantities of material being withdrawn. Taking the time to smooth the way for the sudden appearance of thousands of volumes that need to be handled once a rightsizing project commences will pay off by avoiding unexpected surprises.

Library administrators should be very careful not to create conflict-of-interest situations when disposing of unwanted material. It is natural that in some instances librarians (or faculty members) will agree that certain books should be withdrawn based on low use or obsolescence, but they might also be interested in acquiring some of those books for their personal or professional collections. It would be wise to take proactive steps to avoid preferential treatment in these situations. If the library sells books individually (e.g., book sale, bookshop, online sales), it should handle these withdrawn books like any others; the interested party can buy or bid fairly along with other potential buyers. There should be no opportunity for early purchase, special prices, or outright donation. Not only is there an ethical side to this issue, but also potentially a legal one.

GETTING STARTED

Once the library administration names the project manager and gives the go-ahead for a rightsizing project, it may be tempting to plunge into action immediately. However, the wiser approach is to take the time to lay the groundwork before withdrawing a single volume, even with the pressure of a construction deadline looming. Careful preplanning results in faster and smoother progress when the work begins.

The project manager considers the following points and takes steps to ensure that the appropriate decisions have been made and documented, and that adequate resources are in place before starting. This book addresses many of these topics in more detail elsewhere, but starting to think about the local solutions to these issues helps the manager to understand the project's "moving parts" and to begin formulating the best approach. Here is the project management checklist.

Policy

Has the withdrawal policy, either as part of the collection policy or as a stand-alone document, been written or updated? Is it posted on the library's Internet site with the date of most recent approval?

Rightsizing Plan

Has the administration or other group written the rightsizing plan? Without a document that clearly states the project's expected outcomes and the resources available for it, the manager and other librarians or staff may not feel entirely sure of the administration's support and commitment to the project.

Communication

Has the administration communicated the importance of the upcoming project to the library employees? Are supervisors aware that their staff may be participating in this priority effort? Are the librarians aware that they may be asked to review print retention candidate lists and are expected to turn the work around promptly? If other stakeholders will be informed about the project, what are the plans for doing so?

Staffing

Who will work on the project in its various stages? Will temporary staff be hired for any part of the work? Do permanent staff and their supervisors understand their roles in the project and understand its priority? If some librarians or staff seem reluctant to accept the need for rightsizing, what steps have been taken to offer further explanations? Are there backup staff to handle all functions in case primary staff members are unexpectedly unavailable? Will staff work in their own location only, or can some staff be shared among several locations? Schedule meetings to cover these points and answer questions.

Deadlines

Does any part of the project face a deadline? A written time line ensures that the deadline will be met. Even if there is no fixed deadline, it is important to develop milestones to help keep the project moving.

Type of Material

Will the project focus on journals, books, or other material? If multiple types of material have been targeted for rightsizing, are there reasons why one type should be handled first? What special concerns arise if multiple types must be addressed simultaneously?

Location of Material

Is the material in one location or in many? Are there reasons to begin at one particular location, or can work progress in several locations simultaneously?

Storage

If the library has a storage facility or other storage areas, how will they be involved in the project? Is part of the plan to reduce the amount of material in the storage facility, or is the facility excluded from the rightsizing project? Is one of the project objectives to identify material to withdraw from the active collections as well as to identify titles to transfer to storage, or only one of these actions?

Targets

Are there any targets (e.g., number of books or number of linear feet in the journal stacks) that the project must reach or exceed?

Criteria for Books

First, what material will be *excluded* from the project? Typical materials to exclude will be titles in special collections and archives, government documents, local interest titles, items on reserve, books in the reference collection, maps, etc. Does the library have collections of distinction that should remain intact and, if so, what are the protected call numbers? The remaining titles make up the potential withdrawal candidate pool. If the library previously participated in a distributed print retention project with consortial partners, it is important to exclude any titles that it agreed to keep as part of that earlier collaborative project.

Next, decide what attributes determine which titles will remain in the pool. Attributes usually include variables such as publications before a certain date, circulation thresholds, whether the title is the last copy in a geographical location or consortium, and varying thresholds regarding the number of copies held by other groups of libraries. The section below on workflow for books will address these points more fully.

Criteria for Journals

Is perpetual access electronic availability the only criterion? Are there exceptions, such as journals specifically about the local state or region, or journals in a certain location or subject area? How will the library handle instances of "gap years" between backfile sets and subscriptions? (This chapter's upcoming section on workflow for journals will address these points more fully.)

Criteria for Nonprint Material

Which nonprint material will be included? Do the same thresholds apply as for books? Are there some formats, such as VHS tapes or CD-ROMs, that the library wants to discard completely? If so, what viewing equipment can be removed as well?

Consortial Considerations

Is the library undertaking a rightsizing project in partnership with other libraries in a region or consortium, or is the library acting only on its own behalf? Even if the latter, the library should take consortial holdings into consideration when making local print retention decisions. For example, a library should keep a title, no matter how neglected locally, if it is the last copy in the consortium or region.

Hiring a Consultant

Using a consultant's expertise in developing monograph withdrawal candidate lists allows a library to factor in many more variables than are possible using in-house resources. If the scale of a rightsizing project encompasses tens of thousands of book titles and if the library also wants to compare its collection against those of other libraries, then hiring a consultant is a wise investment. For libraries in a consortial print retention plan, employing a consultant to compile withdrawal candidate lists not only produces better and more consistent results, but also spreads the costs among the members. Look for a consultant who already has experience with print retention projects, can provide samples of decision points and withdrawal candidate lists, has an established relationship with the bibliographic utility that the library uses so that the local collection can be compared with regional and peer partners, and has references from similarly sized institutions that have recently undertaken a similar project.

Whether the library develops its own book withdrawal candidate lists or hires a consultant to produce them, the manager reviews sample results before ordering the full run. Sample results include both a summary sheet with aggregate totals, such as the number of books that meet the criteria, and a sample of what the final lists will look like. At this stage it is still possible to adjust criteria.

Reviewers

Are librarians comfortable relying on the criteria to produce actionable withdrawal lists, or do they want to review titles before staff pull books from the shelves? All titles, or some titles? If there will be review, the project manager establishes a reasonable time frame for list reviews. Who reviews which lists? Are there cases in which multiple librarians should review some lists?

Perpetual Access Journals

The project manager works with the collections team to develop an initial list of publishers and aggregators from whom the library has licensed journal backfiles. The electronic resources librarian contacts the publishers to confirm that the library has perpetual access rights to the journal backfiles (and frontfiles, if applicable). The vendors supply a list that should, at a minimum, provide titles, as well as coverage years and volumes.

Journal List Preparation

Who will prepare journal withdrawal candidate lists? The vendors' lists need to be enhanced with local holdings and location information, as well as with call numbers if the library shelves periodicals that way. If librarians will review the lists to make final retention decisions, then the lists should include a recommended action for each title. The staff who will conduct and record the lookups may need training and their work may need spot checking, at least at first. Who will do this?

Procedures

The manager drafts procedures for various steps of the process as needed. Even if procedures already exist for some processes, they may need to be adapted for handling material in batch mode and on a larger scale than usual.

Supplies and Equipment

What tools do staff need to carry out the project? Are there enough book carts, for example? If a lot of volumes are destined for the remote storage facility, should the manager order extra boxes?

Disposal of Withdrawn Material

Where will the withdrawn material ultimately go? What arrangements need to be made in advance to handle large quantities of withdrawn items? If the journal volumes go to recycling, what is the procedure for sending them in containers that will not be inadvertently left in public places?

Pilot Lists and Procedures

The manager chooses a short list or extracts a small portion from a larger list to test procedures. Staff and colleagues who participate in the pilots can provide suggestions for improving procedures.

Statistics

Does the administration want a separate count of material withdrawn as part of the rightsizing project, or will these figures be captured as part of normal operations? For journals, should titles be counted as well as volumes and, if so, should they only be counted when all print volumes are withdrawn? Is there a reason to record the number of feet freed on the shelves? How will these statistics be captured, maintained, and reported?

The following three sections address the major types of material that make up a library rightsizing project, the decisions that need to be made about each type, and the elements of the rightsizing process. They identify the steps that need to occur and the order in which they should occur to move through all the stages from withdrawal criteria development through material disposal. They suggest ways to manage the workflow, although the project manager can certainly adapt them as needed.

The manager should take time to become familiar enough with the workflows to make suggestions for streamlining or process improvement that will increase efficiency. This task can be a delicate one, because work on the various stages of rightsizing projects cuts across many departmental boundaries. A manager whose main affiliation is with one department, say reference, exercises the skills of a career diplomat to reach consensus on processing paths that go to subject specialists, technical services staff, branch library supervisors, storage e-facility personnel, and the workers who take boxes of withdrawn material to the campus recycling center. The importance of cross-departmental cooperation is another reason why it is important that library administrators not only encourage buy-in from library stakeholders but also empower the project manager with the authority and resources to confer with colleagues to reach consensus on new or adapted procedures.

MANAGING WORKFLOW: JOURNALS

If the library has the luxury of addressing one format at a time, choosing journals for the first rightsizing stage is the best approach.

Selecting print journals for withdrawal presents a different challenge than for books. Most books that are discarded from a collection and then later determined to be useful can be replaced relatively easily. The same is not always true for journals. A journal, by definition, consists of multiple articles published in multiple issues over time. Even when they are focused around a central theme for a special issue, some articles in an issue inevitably receive greater attention and use than others. One cannot pick and choose which articles to keep and which to discard based on use or citation analysis; by withdrawing the whole issue, volume, or run, they all disappear. Replacing them in print will be both difficult and expensive. Replacing them with the electronic equivalent, if available, often means buying the entire backfile of a single title or, in many cases, buying it as part of a backfile bundle.

The availability of the perpetual access digital equivalent from certain publishers and vendors is the trigger that leads individual libraries to undertake withdrawal projects and consortia to make efforts to retain complete print runs of titles, either in designated joint storage facilities, or as part of a distributed retention plan whereby each member agrees to keep specific titles for a specific period of time on behalf of the entire membership. Other members can then withdraw their duplicating journal runs, confident not only that they enjoy stable electronic access to the content, but also that at least one member of group holds backup print.

Today, many of the issues surrounding the print retention of journals can be solved by answering the question, "Is the backfile available electronically and, if so, can my library buy or license it with perpetual access and resource sharing rights?" If the answer is "yes" and the library buys a big package of journal backfiles from the publisher, the dilemma is solved and the print can be discarded—with some caveats, which will be discussed below.

However, the answer is "no" for many titles for a variety of reasons. Some small, specialized publishers do not yet issue their titles electronically or, if they do, have not yet digitized their backfiles. A few publishers currently refuse to offer perpetual access rights or resource sharing rights, either of which would (or *should*) be a deal breaker for most libraries that want to license an electronic subscription or backfile. Some journals ceased publication years ago and have little relevance today, so the chance of commercial digitization is currently remote. Other titles, such as older newspapers, may only be available as part of a larger package; the librarians may only be interested in the local or regional paper and do not want to pay for a large package of titles that their patrons will seldom use.

In general, journal titles are more likely than books to be available in electronic format from a commercial source. Publishers can more easily interest librarians in buying journal backfiles than in buying bundles of older book titles. Major reasons include users being far more comfortable using electronic journal articles than reading entire e-books, and the fact that withdrawing journal volumes frees up much more library space than removing a few hundred books.

Librarians approaching a print journal rightsizing project proceed in two phases. First, they look at what journals they already hold electronically, or are just about to license in that format. They then withdraw the print journals based on those lists, bearing in mind any participation in a consortial print retention initiative. Second, they examine the remaining journal titles and make more time-consuming retention decisions about material that is either unavailable electronically or not of sufficient interest or value to replace with electronic backfiles. This second stage may involve some consortial coordination and should include checking to be sure that sufficient copies exist elsewhere.

Selecting journals for which the library has perpetual access backfiles accomplishes several important objectives. First, withdrawing these print journals does not diminish any access to content. Second, patrons and librarians alike are almost unanimously comfortable using electronic journal articles. Finally, the removal of journal runs has the virtue of freeing up hundreds of feet of shelf space relatively quickly.

It bears reemphasizing that librarians should check their licenses to be certain that they hold perpetual access rights to any journal content before withdrawing print. Why is perpetual access important? Licenses with perpetual access clauses usually indicate that the publisher or vendor assumes the responsibility for migrating content to new technology in the future. In addition, the vendor or publisher undertakes to deposit files with an archiving service like Portico, LOCKSS, or CLOCKSS so that if the company fails, archival copies are available for its customers.

If the library's license does not include perpetual access rights, the publisher can withdraw all access to a journal title if the library stops subscribing to the current issues. Thus librarians cutting e-journal subscription titles in the face of a budget crisis might find that not only do current issues stop, but access to decades of electronic backfiles also suddenly disappears. In addition, because many journal aggregator packages do not include perpetual access, some content may come and go as publishers add or drop titles or change coverage dates. Therefore, it would be unwise to base withdrawal decisions on these aggregators' title lists.

The bare outline of the journal withdrawal process displays a deceptively easy process: buy the perpetual access backfile and withdraw the print:

1. Buy e-journal backfile or select previously purchased backfile.
2. Obtain title list from publisher.
3. Annotate title list to include library locations and holdings.
4. Ask the subject specialist to review withdrawal candidates (optional).
5. Update catalog records (locally and with bibliographic utility).
6. Pull volumes from shelves.
7. Dispose of volumes.

Alas, things are never quite as easy as they should be. Although these seven steps define the process in a nutshell, there are many caveats to keep in mind.

Before designing the journal workflow the manager determines how two important processes will be handled.

The first question involves tracking the number of pieces withdrawn. In many libraries, staff count the number of withdrawn items when they pull items off the shelves. These statistics are usually compiled annually and reported in various places, such as in the library's annual report and, for research libraries, to the Association of Research Libraries. The project manager should check with the administration in advance to ask if additional project statistics should be kept, such as the number of titles withdrawn, if these are not already captured as a part of routine collection maintenance. The administration may also require that statistics unique to the project not be rolled in with the usual annual totals.

Second, many libraries only update their journal holdings with their bibliographic utility a few times a year. A library in the midst of a rightsizing project that includes journals should consider making these updates more frequently for several reasons. One is that its own patrons may search the utility's database and note local availability from the information there. Another is that the library's resource sharing partners use the journal holdings information in the utility's database to make decisions about where to send interlibrary loan requests. In addition, if the interlibrary loan department is a member of any other resource sharing service or group with which it shares the library's serial holdings, then more frequent updates should be made with these organizations, too. It is both time-consuming and frustrating to process ILL requests that e-holdings information shows as available only to find that the volumes were withdrawn six months previously.

Withdrawing JSTOR Journals

This section covers the process of withdrawing JSTOR titles. It serves as a model for journal print retention decisions and workflow, and can be adapted for withdrawing perpetual access journal titles from other publisher or vendor lists, or for withdrawing journals for which there is no electronic equivalent.

Starting with JSTOR titles is an easy way to begin journal withdrawals and to test procedures. JSTOR is a trusted source. Its Arts and Sciences collections cover a wide range of subjects (humanities, social sciences, science, and business), so many locations on a multibranch campus will see some reduction of print titles during the withdrawal process. A number of journal print retention projects have undertaken to build complete runs of JSTOR titles, some of them verified to the page level. There are enough retained copies of JSTOR titles that librarians need not worry that they might be discarding scarce titles. JSTOR titles are "safe" to withdraw.

Choosing JSTOR as a first step or pilot project also helps staff work through all the steps involved in a journal withdrawal project using one of the best-prepared vendor lists available. When later faced with less elegant lists, having a smoothly working local workflow in place will make the job easier.

It may be useful to explore the Decision-Support Tool for JSTOR-Digitized Journals and the accompanying instructional guide at the Ithaka S+R site (www.sr.ithaka.org/research-publications/what-withdraw-print-collec tions-management-wakedigitization). This tool helps librarians decide which JSTOR titles might be local withdrawal candidates; for example, it suggests that some image-heavy titles might be considered for local retention in print because the digital versions may not be an acceptable substitute.

The steps for processing any journal backfile are very similar; differences between JSTOR and single-publisher lists are noted below.

The most important step in a journal rightsizing project is setting up the spreadsheet correctly. Time spent ensuring that information is captured and presented accurately will save hours of troubleshooting further downstream. It is also a task that is best assigned to one or two people. Developing each list should be the sole responsibility of one person, even if several others assist with looking up and recording local information.

The JSTOR website provides accurate and up-to-date title and holding lists that are easy to download into Excel. There are two major caveats with the JSTOR file. First, by its nature, currently published titles have a moratorium of between three and seven years (varying by title) that JSTOR calls the *moving wall*. This moratorium on recently published issues allows publishers to sell subscriptions for current content. Every year JSTOR adds another year of issues to its backfile and the moving wall moves ahead one year. Second, although the master title list at the JSTOR site lists every title available from JSTOR, a particular library may not have subscriptions to all the collections. For instance, the library might not have bought the Irish collection, or may not be up-to-date with all the Arts and Sciences collections. After downloading the master title list into Excel, it is easy to sort by collection name and delete titles from any collections that the library has not bought. (It is also possible to download collection title lists one at a time.)

The JSTOR title file is one of the easiest to work with. It is well arranged, and includes standard numbers like ISSNs. For each title, it clearly indicates both the duration of the moving wall and the years covered at the time of the download. See figure 4.1 for an example of part of the JSTOR title file.

FIGURE 4.1.

JSTOR List #1: Sample Extract Downloaded from the JSTOR Site, before Library-Added Details

Publication Title	Print Identifier	Date First Issue Online	Number First Volume Online	Number First Issue Online	Date Last Issue Online	Number Last Volume Online	Number Last Issue Online	Publisher Name
Academe	0190-2946	2/1/1979	65	1	11/1/2010	96	6	American Association of University Professors
Acadiensis	0044-5851	10/1/1971	1	1	7/1/2010	39	2	Acadiensis: Journal of the History of the Atlantic Region
Accounting Review	0001-4826	3/1/1926	1	1	11/1/2008	83	6	American Accounting Association
Acta Musicologica	0001-6241	1/1/1931	3	1	1/1/2010	82	2	International Musicological Society
Acta Sociologica	0001-6993	1/1/1955	1	1	12/1/2010	53	4	Sage Publications, Ltd.
Acta Turistica	0353-4316	12/1/1989	1	2	12/1/2011	23	2	Faculty of Economics and Business, University of Zagreb
Afers Internacionals	0212-1786	4/1/1982		0	4/1/1985		6	CIDOB
Africa Spectrum	0002-0397	1/1/1966	1	1	1/1/2010	45	3	Institute of African Affairs at GIGA, Hamburg/Germany
Africa Today	0001-9887	4/1/1954	1	1	12/1/2010	57	2	Indiana University Press
African Affairs	0001-9909	7/1/1944	43	172	10/1/2006	105	421	Oxford University Press, The Royal African Society
African American Review	1062-4783	4/1/1992	26	1	12/1/2009	43	4	Indiana State University, St. Louis University
African Arts	0001-9933	10/1/1967	1	1	12/1/2008	41	4	UCLA James S. Coleman African Studies Center
African Music	0065-4019	1/1/1954	1	1	1/1/2008	8	2	International Library of African Music
African Studies Bulletin	0568-1537	4/1/1958	1	1	12/1/1969	12	3	African Studies Association
African Studies Review	0002-0206	4/1/1970	13	1	12/1/2010	53	3	African Studies Association
Afro-Hispanic Review	0278-8969	1/1/1982	1	1	10/1/2010	29	2	William Luis
Agni	1046-218X	1/1/1988		26	1/1/2011		74	Agni
Agni Review	0191-3352	1/1/1972		1	1/1/1987		24/25	Agni
Agricultural History	0002-1482	1/1/1927	1	1	10/1/2010	84	4	Agricultural History Society
Agricultural History Review	0002-1490	1/1/1953	1	1	1/1/2008	56	2	British Agricultural History Society

It will be helpful to refer to figure 4.2 while reviewing the next few pages. It is an example of part of a JSTOR list that has been edited to include new columns, and it contains some added local holdings information recorded for the first few titles.

FIGURE 4.2.
JSTOR List #2: Sample Working List with Added Columns and Local Holdings Information

Publication Title	ISSN	Location	Storage	Holdings	Recommend	First Issue Date
Academe	0190-2946	Main		v.65(1979)-2014	keep 2008+	2/1/1979
Academy of Management Journal	0001-4273	Business	v.6(1963)-v.26(1983)	v.27(1984)-2014	keep 2008+	3/1/1963
Acadiensis	0044-5851		v.1(1971)-v.21(1991)		wd all	10/1/1971
Accounting Review	0001-4826	Business	v.1(1926)-v.61(1986)	v. 62(1987)-2014	keep 2008+	3/1/1926
Acta Musicologa	0001-6241	Music	v.1(1931)-v. 71(2001)	v.72(2002)-2014	keep 2008+	1/1/1931
Acta Oeconomica	0001-6373	Business	v.1(1966)-21(1986)	v. 22(1987)-1995	wd all	1/1/1966
Acta Turistica	0353-4316	online only				12/1/1989
Advances in Applied Probability	0001-8678	Math		v.1(1969)-2014	keep 2008+	4/1/1969
Advances in Applied Probability	0001-8678	Math - **mf**		v.1(1969)-1968	wd all	4/1/1969
Aevum	0001-9593	online only				1/1/1927
Africa Today	0001-9887		v.46(1999)-2006		wd all	4/1/1954
Agricultural History	0002-1482		v.1(1927)-1999		wd all	1/1/1927
Aldine	2151-4186	online only				1871-01-01
American Biology Teacher	0002-7685	Science		v.1(1938)-2010 + publisher	wd all	10/1/1938
American College Bulletin	2163-7652					10/20/1917
American Economic Review	0002-8282					3/1/1911
American Economist	0569-4345					5/1/1960
American Ethnologist	0094-0496					2/1/1974
American Fern Journal	0002-8444					8/1/1910
American Historical Review	0002-8762					1895-10-01
American Humor	0193-7146					4/1/1974

JSTOR list preparation proceeds as follows:

1. Download the master title file from JSTOR and save it in Excel.
2. Name the file JSTOR1. Because of its ongoing nature, both in terms of new titles being added and the moving wall coverage changing each year, it is likely that the project manager will revisit the JSTOR title list every few years to pick up new titles and volumes that can be withdrawn. When the next JSTOR list is created in perhaps three to five years, it can be called JSTOR2. See figure 4.3 for suggested file naming conventions.
3. Sort the file by the JSTOR collection names. Delete lines for collections that the library does not have.
4. Resort alphabetically by title.
5. At the top of the worksheet, include the file name and the date that it was downloaded. The previous file, JSTOR1, remains saved as a backup. Save this file as JSTOR1Master.
6. Using file JSTOR1Master, insert some new columns after the ISSN column. Label them Location; Storage (or the name of the storage facility if there is one and if the plan includes withdrawing material from it); Holdings; Call Number (if call numbers are needed to locate journals); and Recommendation. If the storage facility uses location codes, and if these will be captured during the lookup process, add another column for Storage Location Number. Figure 4.2 shows a sample spreadsheet with one storage location, but if there are several storage locations from which volumes may be withdrawn, create a separate column for each one.
7. Save JSTOR1Master as JSTOR1wc (working copy). No further changes are made to the master file. It is helpful to keep the file in its pristine form as a backup in case something happens to the working copy.

Variation: If a copy list is so long that several people will be looking up location information for it, break the working copy list into

FIGURE 4.3.

Suggested File Naming Conventions (JSTOR Example)

JSTOR1	Title file from publisher/aggregator
JSTOR1Master	File sorted by title; new columns added
JSTOR1wc	Working copy used for recording locations, etc.
JSTOR1final	Final copy with all locations and recommendations
JSTOR1music, JSTOR1mainC	Sublists by location
JSTOR1scienceArev	Sublist after subject specialist's review

sublists of about one hundred titles each. These lists might be named JSTOR1wc1, JSSTOR1wc2, and so on. Assign one list at a time to staff. The advantage is that with several people looking up locations and call numbers, the work will go quickly. The disadvantage is that the reviewers (if any) will receive several smaller lists rather than one larger list. (It may become too complicated for the manager to try to reassemble the multiple completed sublists with recorded location information back into one long file, sort by library location, and then divide the long file again by location.)

8. Using JSTOR1wc, look up location information. If the library's catalog or discovery layer can be searched efficiently by ISSN, cutting and pasting this number assures quick and easy matches. Although lookup work can be assigned to other staff for other kinds of journal lists, for JSTOR lists this work should be carried out by the manager or assigned to an experienced employee trained in the tasks described below, for reasons that will become clear.

9. These are the possible results of a search for titles on a JSTOR list:

    a. *The library has the JSTOR electronic title only, and no equivalent print.* Staff newly assigned to look-up tasks should annotate these as "online only" in the location column so that a supervisor can spot check these later. Experienced staff can delete these titles. In figure 4.2, the title *Acta Turista* is an example of a JSTOR title that the library holds in the online version only.

    b. *The title is held in print in a single location other than storage.* Enter the location name in the Location column and the holdings in the Holdings column. See *Academe* in figure 4.2 for an example.

    c. *The title is only held in print in storage.* Figure 4.2 shows *Acadiensis* as an example.

    d. *The title is held in both an active library location and in storage.* Record this information in the appropriate columns. See *Academy of Management Journal* in figure 4.2 for an example.

    e. *The title is held in multiple active library locations.* Insert a new line on the spreadsheet and copy the information about the title. Then add the additional location and holdings information on the new line. See *Advances in Applied Probability* in figure 4.2 for an example. It is important to make a new line because each instance of the title may require different actions. In this example, a few of the print volumes will be retained, but all of the microfilm holdings will be withdrawn. Also, the list will be sorted later by location, so if a title has a run in both the Science Library and the Main Library, for example, it is important that each instance of the holdings appears on a separate line.

f. *The title appears on the JSTOR list, but it does not appear in the catalog as an electronic journal, although there may or may not be print volumes.* Highlight these lines consistently in one color. The most likely explanation is that this title was not activated for some reason. At the end of the lookup phase, the manager can assign these highlighted titles to one of the electronic resources staff to double-check the activation status. Once the titles are activated, they should be processed in a group according to the steps outlined below.

10. Processing notes include the following:

   a. Cut and paste the holdings statement from the catalog into the Holdings column (or into the Storage column if that is the correct location). If the holdings statement is very long due to scattered holdings, ask technical services staff if it would be acceptable to shorten the statement, for example from the original v.125(1962), v.126:no.2(1963)-v.127(1964), v.128:no.3(1965), v.129:no.2(1966)-v.127(1964), v.128:no.3(1965), v.129:no.2(1966)-v.130:no.1(1967), v.130:no.3(1967)-v.157:no.4(1994), v.158:no.2(1995)-v.169(2006–2007)-v.170:no.1(2007), v.170:no.3(2008) to something like: v.125(1962)-v.170:no.3(2008) [edited].

   b. Add any special notes to the holdings statement such as "[bound with v. 16 of Journal of X]" or "+ indexes" using red text.

   c. While looking for print holdings, also check for any e-journal holdings that bridge the gap between the JSTOR moving wall and the present. For example, record the holdings as "v.3(1981)-v.30:no.8(2009) + publisher" if the library holds a perpetual access e-subscription to the same title and if that access bridges the gap, in this case between 2009 and the present. In this particular case, at the time of lookup the JSTOR moving wall stopped at 2007 for this title. The library has print through 2009. Without the note about the subscription, the library should withdraw 1981–2007 in print, but keep 2008 and 2009 because JSTOR content did not yet extend that far. However, the note about the publisher perpetual access e-subscription that bridged the moving wall means that the library can safely withdraw all print volumes; JSTOR covers 1979–2007, and the publisher covers 1995 onward. It is important to be sure that the e-coverage is from a publisher's perpetual access subscription and not from an aggregator's collection, which may change without notice or which may not offer complete coverage of a title. *American Biology Teacher* shows an example of this type of note in figure 4.2.

d. Add any necessary recommendations. Having just established the print holdings and any permanent e-coverage, the person conducting the lookups makes a recommendation in the next column. The two most common recommendations are "wd all" if JSTOR or JSTOR+publisher covers the library's entire print run; or "keep YEAR+" where YEAR the date from which print volumes should be kept because there is as yet no JSTOR e-coverage for them and there is also no stable publisher coverage (e.g., "keep 2014+"). For convenience, the manager may select a year five or six years in the past as the standard year to use, except in cases where the moving wall is longer and thus the year must be set further back to ensure that the library does not lose any content. The manager should also be alert for cases in which the library has a current print subscription. It may be prudent to choose the same year five or six years in the past for keeping print issues of current subscriptions (the print holdings are up to date). Occasionally the manager may recommend keeping a title or transferring it to the storage facility (if there is one). For example, the author suggested storing some volumes of *Hoosier Folklore* from the 1940s. Even with JSTOR coverage, preserving the print volumes of an in-state publication about local cultural heritage seemed like a good idea. Very occasionally, there will be an odd gap in the JSTOR coverage in which case the print volumes should be kept or transferred to storage. It is because of the need to make recommendations for JSTOR titles that it makes sense for the manager or a few specially trained assistants to conduct all the lookups and to make the recommendations title by title while the information is fresh in his or her mind. Looking at someone else's notes about holdings and making the recommendations later are a lengthier process.

11. Review. If the librarians have indicated that they want to review the list before withdrawals begin, then the manager inserts a new column after Recommendation called Instructions, giving subject specialists a place to make notes about any titles for which something other than the recommendation should occur.

12. Create final list. Copy the working-copy list as the final list, e.g., JSTOR1final. Archive the working copy version. It is now a permanent record of the file with all the location and recommendation information.

13. Create sublists. Sort the final file by location. Some locations will hold relatively few titles so it may be easiest to start with them. Starting with JSTOR1final, save it as, for example, JSTOR1business. On this new file, delete all but the titles in the business library. Edit the

worksheet header to indicate that this is the business sublist. Do the same for other locations, starting each time with `JSTOR1final` and naming each sublist to reflect the main list from which it was derived as well as the subject or location of the journals on the sublist. Some sublists can be very long. For example, the JSTOR sublist for a main library might be several hundred lines long. Trying to divide these up by subject specialties might be very time consuming and, in some cases, very difficult for multidisciplinary titles. One solution is to break the long sublists further into shorter lists of about 100 titles each, calling them something like `JSTOR1mainA`, `JSTOR1mainB`, and so on, and then posting the files on a shared drive so that all the reviewers can access them. It is best to post one file at a time and set a firm deadline about six weeks in the future for each posted file. The deadline and necessary instructions can be sent to the group via e-mail. When the first deadline passes, take the file down, post the next one, and contact colleagues with the new due date for the next list. Figure 4.4 shows a sample sublist for a specific location.

14. There will be some titles for which there are holdings only in the storage facility. Because these are usually, by definition, older titles, ask the librarians if they want to review this part of the list. If so, divide these titles in sublists by subject (based on the titles) and send them out for review as suggested above.

15. Contact reviewers. For longer sublists, it is courteous to contact the individual subject specialists in advance to ask if this is a convenient time to send a journal review file with a review due date a month in the future. If the colleague responds to indicate that he would have more available time in a few months, make a note to send the list later. Unless there is a compelling reason why the review must take place almost immediately, try to accommodate colleagues' schedules. For lists of up to about twenty titles, it is usually fine to send it as an e-mail attachment without a prior announcement. The e-mail that accompanies the list should have a subject line such as "JSTOR1business review list–due July 1." For the text, develop a standard message that can be slightly edited to suit each subject and deadline date. Provide clear instructions, restate the deadline, and invite the recipient to ask questions as necessary. See figure 4.5 for sample wording for the message.

16. Enter the sublist in a tracking file with its name, the reviewer's name or initials, and the date sent. See figure 4.6 for a sample journal list tracking file.

17. Mark the list's final version. Each time a sublist goes to a reviewer, return to the final version of the list and mark those titles by highlighting them. The highlighting provides a visual clue that action is being taken on those titles.

FIGURE 4.4.

Sample Journal Title Sublist Sorted by Location

Publication Title	Location	Repository	Holdings	Recommendation
Biological Bulletin	LIFE		v.212(2007)-v.223(2012)	wd all
Copeia	LIFE		2005-2012	keep 2008+
Estuaries and Coasts	LIFE		v.29(2006)-v.34(2011) + publisher	wd all
Human Biology	LIFE	v.1(1929)-v.52(1980)	v.65(1993)-v.79(2007)	wd all
Journal of the History of Biology	LIFE	v.1(1968)-v.17(1984)	v.18(1985)-v.40(2007)	wd all
Journal of the Torrey Botanical Society	LIFE		v.132(2005)-v.140:no.3(2013: July/Sept.)	keep 2008+
Journal of Wildlife Management	LIFE	v.1(1932)-v.48(1984)	v.49(1985)-v.73(2009)	wd all
Kew Bulletin	LIFE	v.14(1960)-v.34(1980)	v.35(1980/1981)-v.66:no.4(2011)	keep 2008+
Madrono	LIFE	v.1(1916)-v.35(1988)	v.36(1989)-v.56(2009)	wd all
Microbial Ecology	LIFE		v.1(1974)-v.54(2007)	wd all
Mycologia	LIFE	v.1 (1909)-v.66 (1974)	v.67(1975)-v.104(2012)	keep 2008+
Physiological and Biochemical Zoology	LIFE		v.72(1999)-v.84:no.1(2011)	keep 2008+
Physiological Zoology	LIFE	v.1 (1928)-v.52 (1979)	v.53(1980)-v.71(1998)	wd all
Plant Cell	LIFE		v.1(1989)-v.23(2011)	wd all
Plant Ecology	LIFE		v.128(1997)-v.133(1997)	wd all
Plant Physiology	LIFE	v.1(1926)-v.76(1984)	v.77(1985)-v.157(2011)	wd all
Planta	LIFE	Bd.1(1927)-122(1975)	Bd.123(1975)-Bd.226(2007)	keep 1927-1933
Rangeland Ecology and Management	LIFE		v.58(2005)-v.62(2009)	wd all
Southwestern Naturalist	LIFE	v.1 (1956)-v.19 (1975)	v.20(1975)-v.54(2009)	wd all
Vegetatio	LIFE	v.1 (1948)-v.63 (1985)	v.64 (1985)-v.127 (1996)	wd all
Weed Science	LIFE		v.16(1968)-v.57(2009)	wd all
Wildlife Society Bulletin	LIFE	v.1(1973)-v.13(1985)	v.14(1986)-v.34(2006) [edited]	wd all
Wilson Journal of Ornithology	LIFE		v.118(2006)-v.121(2009)	wd all

18. Follow up. If about two weeks have passed since a review list's due date, send a gently worded reminder note to the subject specialist. If there are extenuating circumstances why the list will be late, try to accommodate them. In a major rightsizing effort, each subject specialist will review many different lists and will appreciate polite reminders from a manager who accommodates the occasional need for extending deadlines. Figure 4.7 suggests the wording for a reminder note.

FIGURE 4.5.

Sample E-mail Message to a Colleague about a Journal List Review

Subject: JSTOR1business review list – due July 1

Message: I have attached a file called JSTOR1business. It contains 73 journal titles with holdings in the Business Library, or in both the Business Library and the Storage Annex. The spreadsheet shows the print holdings for each title. The Recommendation column suggests a withdrawal action based on JSTOR holdings plus any other perpetual access e-holdings, if available.

If you would prefer an action other than the one suggested in Recommendations, please make a note in the Instructions column.

Please return the annotated list to me by July 1.

I'd be happy to answer any questions.

Thank you.

19. Rename the reviewed list. When a colleague returns `JSTOR1music`, for example, rename it as `JSTOR1musicRev` and continue working from the `Rev` version.

20. Conduct post-review processing. Post-review processing consists of several final steps that culminate with removing volumes from the shelves.

   a. *Reviewer notes.* The manager checks the returned list for any notes that the reviewer has left. The most common note is a request to leave the print volumes where they are (i.e., do not withdraw them), or to move a run of volumes to the storage facility rather than discarding them. The subject specialist may also want to retain the major journal for a discipline, or may feel that the digital rendition of fine lines in geological drawings or in reproductions of artworks are not an acceptable substitute for the print. The manager generally accommodates these requests. If one reviewer marks an unusually high number of titles for retention or there is a serious space crisis that precludes making more than a few exceptions, the manager should follow up with the reviewer and, if necessary, the reviewer's supervisor.

   b. *Titles in storage.* Many sublists contain a combination of titles for which the volumes reside only in one active location, or only in the storage facility, or in both an active location *and* in the storage facility (usually a split run, but sometimes titles duplicated in

FIGURE 4.6.

Sample Journal List Tracking File

List Name	Look Ups	Reviewer	Storage	Tech Services	Circ Supervisor	Finished
JSTOR1art	Done	HK 5/13, rem 7/2	7/15	7/22	7/25	8/5
JSTOR1business	Done	DB 5/21	5/29	6/9	6/15, rem 7/29	7/7
JSTOR1mainA	Done	RD 5/21	6/8	6/17	6/24	
JSTOR1mainB	Done	RD 6/19	7/12			
Wiley1a	PF 7/2					
Wiley1b	SY 7/2					
Wiley1c	FR 7/2					
Wiley1cStorage	Done	n/a	7/19	7/22	n/a	7/24
Wiley1cMain	Done	GC 7/19				
Wiley1cScience	Done	WW 7/19	7/30	8/5	8/10	
Wiley1d	DW 7/2					
Wiley1e	FR 7/21					
Wiley1f						
Wiley1g						
JSTOR1mainC	n/a	RD 7/29				
ACS1a	LT 7/6	PW 8/1	8/15			
ACS1b	LT 8/3					
JSTOR1scienceA	Done	WW 8/2				
Springer1a						
Springer1b						
Springer1c						
Springer1d						
Springer1e						
Springer1f						
Springer1g						
Springer1h						

whole or in part). It is critical to know if the staff in the storage facility need to see lists with storage titles *before* they go to technical services in order to look up any shelf location information that will be lost if the title records and their associated barcodes are withdrawn first. If so, send the list to storage staff *first* with instructions to locate the volumes and remove them from the shelves, and then to report back to the manager when this has been done. Storage staff can be sent the whole sublist; they will

FIGURE 4.7.

Sample Reminder e-mail to a Colleague about a Journal List Review

---

Subject: Reminder: JSTOR1business review list – due July 1

Message: Just a quick reminder about this journal review list that I sent you on May 29 and that was due two weeks ago on July 1.

I'm resending instructions in case you need them. Please let me know if you have any questions.

Thank you.

I have attached a file called JSTOR1business. It contains 73 journal titles with holdings in the Business Library, or in both the Business Library and the Storage Annex. The spreadsheet shows the print holdings for each title. The Recommendation column suggests a withdrawal action based on JSTOR holdings plus any other perpetual access e-holdings, if available.

If you would prefer an action other than the one suggested in Recommendations, please make a note in the Instructions column.

Please return the annotated list to me by July 1.

I'd be happy to answer any questions.

Thank you.

---

ignore any titles that are held in other locations. In most cases, the entire storage run will be withdrawn, but it is worth taking the time in advance to check the list and to highlight any cases in which only part of the run is to be withdrawn. Mark the tracking file with the date that the list was sent to storage staff and send a reminder note if more than two weeks pass without a response.

c. *Technical services.* After the storage staff report that any volumes in their facility are off the shelves (or the location information noted for later volume removal), the manager then sends the list to technical services staff with instructions to update both the local system and the bibliographic utility that the library uses. Mark the tracking file with this date. Until the staff become familiar with the lists' format, it is worth reminding them to watch the Recommendations column carefully because some titles will be withdrawn in their entirety, whereas others will remain with just a few recent volumes on the shelf. The staff notify the manager when this has been done.

d. *Removing volumes from the shelves.* If the storage staff have already acted on the list, the manager reviews the post-technical services

FIGURE 4.8.
Sample E-mail to a Circulation Supervisor to Pull Journal Volumes
(JSTOR Example)

Subject: JSTOR1artRev – pull & recycle

Message: I have attached a file called JSTOR1artRev.

These journal volumes can be pulled from the shelves and recycled. Please watch the notes in the Recommendation column -- some titles should be pulled in their entirety, but we need to keep a few volumes from other titles.

The art subject specialist has reviewed and approved these withdrawals. The storage staff are acting on any volumes shown in their location. The catalog has already been updated.

Please let me know when you have completed this work.

I'd be happy to answer any questions.

Thank you.

---

list and deletes any titles with volumes that were *only* held in storage, because these have been handled already. The resulting list will now contain titles held at a single library location. This list goes to the circulation supervisor at that library with instructions to remove the volumes from the shelves (some in their entirety and some only partially, as indicated) and to dispose of the withdrawn volumes in the approved manner. Mark the tracking file with this date. The circulation supervisor notifies the manager when this has been done, then the manager notes that the sublist has been completely finished. Figure 4.8 provides a sample e-mail message to a circulation supervisor to begin the volume removal process.

e. *Troubleshooting.* Despite everyone's best efforts, questions are bound to come up at any stage in the process. The manager investigates these and directs the staff's efforts with the ultimate goal of removing volumes from the shelves and being sure that the library's records reflect the changes correctly.

If librarians have agreed that they do not need to review journal lists from JSTOR or from certain publishers, then the manager skips steps concerned with reviews. However, it would still be a good idea to break long lists into sublists of not more than about one hundred titles each. Shorter lists are far less daunting for staff to handle in the various processing stages, although tracking all the sublists through their multiple processing stages then becomes more of a challenge for the manager.

Even if the manager has the luxury of finishing the JSTOR list before moving on to a publisher's journal list, there are many simultaneous sublists in progress. Some librarians may still be reviewing parts of long sublists while other shorter sublists have moved on to later processing stages. Delays are inevitable: people take vacations, fall ill, take sabbaticals, accept other positions, retire, or encounter unexpected life events. Lists may be misplaced or forgotten. It is the manager's responsibility to keep the whole process moving forward and, very probably, to be preparing the next list to start the process anew with more titles. Some managers may also be simultaneously working with lists of books that are candidates for withdrawal.

It may seem redundant to track blocks of titles on the final version of the journal list as well as on a sublist tracking file, but it is very helpful for the manager to follow two separate processes: the assignment of titles from master lists to sublists, and the activity of sublists traveling through several different stages (review, storage action if needed, technical services action, and withdrawal action). Because the manager may be juggling several title lists in the final stage (not to mention setting up new lists), plus assigning sublists to multiple people through multiple stages, it is essential to have some reliable way to determine at a glance where every sublist is and which ones are overdue. With such a system, for example, the manager can avoid swamping one reviewer with multiple lists at the same time. It is also very rewarding to mark off sublists when they have been completely finished.

Unlike some other journal backfiles which are static purchases in that they cover a selection of titles each from volume 1 to some specific date or until the subscription starts, the JSTOR list constantly expands. The earliest collections are closed, meaning that all the titles that will be included in those collections are already present, although for currently published titles the moving wall changes each year. When JSTOR adds a new collection, the backfiles are added to it a few titles at a time over a period of several years. The moving walls for some titles in all the collections change every year as older volumes fall into the date range included in the JSTOR files. Libraries buy additional collections, but may not necessarily add the new ones as soon as they are announced. For these reasons, a JSTOR withdrawal project is not a onetime activity, but one that should be scheduled every few years. The first withdrawal will be a large one. However, subsequent rounds will identify any newly added titles or collections, as well as a few more years from other titles where the moving wall has advanced, thus releasing a few more volumes that can be withdrawn from many titles.

The JSTOR process involves one of the longer lists that the staff will encounter. Most other lists will be smaller and thus easier to manage.

However, when working with long lists, it is helpful to break them into sub-lists even if all the titles are shelved in a single library or if the project is focusing on titles in only one or two locations. In the author's experience, a journal title sublist of no more than about one hundred titles is optimal. The various processing stages take time to complete thoroughly and accurately; adding the complication of handling a massive list can lead to frustration, inaccuracies, and exhaustion. Psychologically, it is much easier to handle each of these tasks in smaller doses so that no one feels overwhelmed. Each of the sublists can be handled in different stages at the same time so that, for example, student assistants might be pulling A to B titles, while catalog clerks update C to D titles, librarians review E to F titles, and the lookup staff work on G to H titles. Besides avoiding unnecessary stress and burnout, staggering the tasks means that if there is a problem in one area, such as the key catalog clerk taking a three-week vacation, other parts of the process continue smoothly and the backlog is minimized.

This JSTOR workflow model can be adapted for title lists from other aggregators that provide backfile coverage from a variety of publishers. The important point is to determine in advance if the library licensed perpetual access rights to the electronic content and, if so, for what exact range of dates and volumes; without this assurance, there is always the possibility that titles may be removed without warning, leaving the library with no immediate access to the content once the print has been withdrawn.

Withdrawing Other Journals

The next target, publisher packages, presents other challenges. Over time, many large publishers acquire some titles from smaller ones and, when they do so, do not always acquire all the digital rights to the back issues. If a library licenses the "complete" electronic backfiles from a publisher, the project manager works with the electronic resources librarian to get the correct list of perpetual access titles. For example, a particular title may have been acquired by the current publisher starting with volume 10. From that volume onward, the current publisher offers perpetual access, but because the original publisher still retains some rights to the earlier content, the access to those first nine volumes is not perpetual. Librarians need to be aware of this fact, and make a conscious decision about whether to take the calculated risk of withdrawing the print volumes for the earlier years. In other cases, new licenses for backfiles include perpetual access rights for all or most titles, but earlier contracts signed for electronic subscriptions might not include these rights.

In other fairly typical circumstances, publishers might license a perpetual access backfile to all their titles from volume one until a specific date, for example, 2000. A library might have had print subscriptions to two-thirds of those titles and might have switched to electronic subscriptions for those titles in 2005. The publisher throws in the gap years of 2001–2004 as part of the backfile deal, but the gap-year backfiles do not include perpetual access because the library never paid for them in the electronic format, either as part of the backfile or on a subscription basis. In this example, the gap only spans three years, but in many cases the gap might be as long as fifteen years. What should the library do? Should it withdraw only the volumes with perpetual access coverage, thus retaining forlorn clusters of a few print volumes for many titles? Should it withdraw the whole run? After all, it has electronic access to the whole run right now, even if a small portion of that access is not perpetual. If some of the subscribed titles should be cut later and e-access for the gap years disappears, at least that gap will be further in the past by then, and interlibrary loan service can fill in when patrons occasionally need articles from those years. Sometimes the library can buy a perpetual access gap-years package, but some publishers bundle these so the library cannot buy the gap years for just the titles it subscribes to, but only a package that includes the rest of the publisher's titles as well. This option may be too expensive. Figure 4.9 provides a graphic representation of the gap-year problem.

There are a number of ways to manage journal withdrawals based on lists of perpetual access titles from the publishers or other vendors. Starting with a publisher- or vendor-supplied list and processing it as in the previous JSTOR example is one method. Several articles provide details about possible methodologies for withdrawing journal titles and volumes based on e-journal lists (Bracke and Martin 2005; Sorensen 2009; Thomas and Shouse 2012). Gallagher and Rathemacher explained a method using information from their library's journal management software, which allowed them to sort titles by call number and to select specific subject areas (medicine and science) as the initial target area for withdrawals; this method offers the option of creating title lists irrespective of publisher (Gallagher and Rathemacher 2012). A locally generated list may be "cleaner" than publishers' lists in the sense that all title changes will be listed separately. However, the list still needs to be checked against print holdings, because libraries have access to many electronic journals for which they do not hold the print equivalent, and the call numbers, holdings statements, and locations (if the library has more than one

FIGURE 4.9.

Example of a Gap in Perpetual Access for a Journal Title

PRINT	v.1(1900)–v.108(2009)		
ELECTRONIC	v.1(1900)–v.95(1996) Backfile perpetual access	1997–2004	2005+ E-subscription, perpetual access

Publisher provides e-access to the 1997–2004
"gap," but it is *not* perpetual access.

location for bound journals) need to be looked up and recorded. If using journal management software for list generation, be sure that the titles are from publishers or vendors providing perpetual access.

Some publisher lists are notorious for lumping all the holdings under the most recent title, which requires that that library staff first notice and then break out the earlier titles so that withdrawal lists match catalog records and provide accurate information for the staff who pull volumes from the shelves. In the following example, the journal title has been changed to conceal the publisher's identity, but it is an actual case that the author encountered and similar to many others like it.

The publisher's list cited *Martian Bulletin of Knitting and Crocheting* with dates between 1911 and 2009. This title appeared in the library's catalog, but with volume 1 starting in 1959, not 1911. Investigation revealed a previous title, *Martian Bulletin of Knitting,* which appeared between 1957 and 1958. Before that, under simply *Bulletin of Knitting,* the journal started in 1911 and ran until 1956. The information on the spreadsheet needed to be updated to show all three titles, all three ranges of volume numbers and dates and, in this case, two call numbers. Without making these changes on the list, staff handling catalog updates or pulling volumes from the shelves would encounter difficulties with records and volumes that would not match the information on the lists.

It is also important to know that for a variety of reasons the electronic holdings will not always match the print holdings exactly. It does not matter if the electronic holdings include some earlier years than the print holdings, but it is critical to pay close attention to determine if the more recent electronic content completely covers the more recent print volumes. Not only is there the possibility of gaps in coverage as explained above, but also journal backfiles may end in, say, 1995, while the print volumes continued until 2008. To avoid losing coverage, staff must take care to note that, in this example, print volumes can be withdrawn through 1995, but 1996 through 2008 must be retained if the library wants to avoid losing content.

Publisher lists usually include all the titles in the journal backfile package, but most libraries will only hold a subset of these in print. The author has found it advantageous to have one person check quickly through the whole list at the outset simply to delete any titles for which the library has electronic access only. The resulting list then contains only titles with print holdings; it can then be assigned, or broken into sublists and then assigned, to the staff who conduct the location lookups. It is somehow more rewarding to find and record holdings for one title after another than it is to look up several titles that turn out to have no local print or microfilm holdings in between every one or two titles that do have local holdings.

Other challenges arise from the gradual transition that publishers and libraries have been making from the traditional print-only subscription model though the print-*and*-electronic phase to the e-journal–only stage. Different publishers are still at different places in this evolution. Some small and specialty presses still issue their journals as print-only. Other publishers offer their serials in both print and electronic versions with subscribers being able to choose one or the other format (or both). Most libraries are moving towards choosing e-only options, but there are still good reasons to want both versions, at least for selected titles. A variation of this model occurs with some publishers who still send both the print and the electronic versions to their institutional subscribers, regardless of whether those subscribers actually want both formats. Many libraries simply discard the print issues as they arrive. Finally, more and more journals have reached the electronic-only stage. At libraries subscribing to thousands of journal titles, some of them through subscription agents, staff have found it difficult to keep up with all the titles switching from print-and-electronic to the option of print-or-electronic. During a rightsizing project, staff will encounter many titles with electronic coverage up through the most current issue, yet the library still subscribes to the print version as well. The middle of a rightsizing project is usually not the best time to try to address the challenge of systematically dropping duplicate print subscriptions in favor of electronic-only ones. It is also not a good idea to withdraw print right up to the current issue in cases where the library still subscribes to the print journal but also has current electronic coverage. For some titles, subject specialists will have made conscious decisions to keep the print subscriptions active; the rightsizing project does not intend to undermine those decisions. The manager makes a decision to keep a certain number of years of print back issues, perhaps three or five, in these cases.

Print volumes corresponding to publisher e-journal backfile lists are also "safe" withdrawals. The very fact that the publishers went to the expense of digitizing these journals means that they know there is considerable demand for the journals, or for the backfile packages as a whole, because many libraries hold those titles in print. Several large research libraries and regional consortia have undertaken to maintain print copies of large portions of these publishers' output.

Working with publishers' lists and with lists from selected aggregators offering perpetual access titles is similar to working with a JSTOR list. The title list is downloaded or requested from the vendor. The spreadsheets can be set up to look similar to the JSTOR lists. The process of looking up holdings and location information is the same, as is making decisions for each title: can all the print volumes be withdrawn because the electronic version covers them completely, or should the library retain some volumes because the coverage, or the perpetual access coverage, is not complete? If the library wants to retain gap-year volumes between the backfile and subscription, should these be transferred to the storage facility rather than left in the active periodical stacks? These lists do not have moving wall considerations, but otherwise processing them is very similar to the JSTOR lists.

A potential second phase in journal print retention work involves working with titles without electronic equivalents, either because the library decides not to get the available backfiles, or because any backfiles do not include perpetual access, or because no electronic equivalent exists at all. These are all low- or no-use titles that can be considered for withdrawal for one or more of the following reasons.

Short or scattered runs. If a more complete run exists within the consortium and there are enough other holding libraries in the country, then these are withdrawal candidates.

Longer runs that are widely held and not needed locally. Foreign language titles often fall into this category, but the library should retain scarce titles.

Titles with all holdings dated before 1923. If the library's holdings are duplicated in full text in projects like Google Books HathiTrust and there are sufficient print copies in other libraries, these are withdrawal candidates.

The manager compiles a list of print journal titles with all the pertinent local and bibliographic information. If government publications with their special considerations will not be considered, they can be deleted from the list (i.e., retained). The list is divided by location. Many long runs can be immediately eliminated if the project focuses on short or scattered runs. However, shorter runs should be examined closely to identify and delete any that are short title changes of a longer title that the library wants to retain. Staff then check the remaining titles, recording findings like perpetual access electronic holdings, consortial holdings, and overall scarcity in the region or country. They note foreign language titles. Will the subject specialists review the withdrawal candidates? The withdrawal candidate list follows a similar path to that described in the JSTOR section above. One variation might be to identify some scarce titles to transfer from active collections to the storage facility.

Ward and Aagard's article details a project to identify and withdraw short and scattered journal runs in a storage facility (Ward and Aagard 2008).

MANAGING WORKFLOW: BOOKS

It is relatively straightforward to determine what to withdraw when working with journal lists, especially if a major criterion is the presence of perpetual access digital equivalents.

Developing withdrawal candidate lists for books is more of an art, and can be fraught with anxiety when librarians propose withdrawing material for which there is no electronic equivalent. See figure 4.10 for the book rightsizing workflow.

For centuries, books have been the containers into which authors gathered, and publishers issued, the results of philosophical, creative, or research endeavors. For many of those centuries books were so expensive that they were issued in small print runs or, before printing, as single items. Over time, research may become outdated, some philosophical ideas are rejected, and fiction or poetry is deemed old-fashioned. The people who own the books decide not to keep them any longer and the number of extant copies dwindles over time. Eventually, institutions holding these titles find that they have one of the few remaining copies of, for example, a tome of tedious sermons. The fact that only a handful of copies exists several centuries later may bestow upon a book an intrinsic value far outweighing the more limited value of its content.

However, what is true about the intrinsic value of one of ten remaining copies of an outdated and otherwise unremarkable eighteenth-century book is not true of an outdated 1950s book published in thousands of copies and collected by hundreds of libraries. Although we cannot predict how the researcher of 2350 will regard the book published in the 1950s, even if only ten physical copies of it exist by that time, we would probably be right in predicting that the future researcher will be just as happy to get what she needs from a digital (or twenty-fourth-century equivalent) copy of that book as today's scholars would be to read the 1750s sermons from *Eighteenth Century Collections Online*. But today we need not wait 300 years before the thousands of copies of millions of books disappear through normal attrition. In fact, if we manage academic libraries, we cannot wait. Even if we did not need the space for other activities, collectively we cannot afford to maintain indefinitely the millions of copies of books that have outlived the major part of their usefulness. If we work collaboratively to maintain and preserve a sufficient number of copies of each title, then most libraries can discard their duplicate copies.

Books in different subject areas may require different withdrawal criteria. Books in science and technology, for example, tend to become obsolete much faster than those in the humanities. A medical book from 1930 almost certainly contains at least some treatment recommendations that now might be considered ineffective at best or harmful at worst. A historical figure's biography published in 1930 may still be very useful today; later scholars might have uncovered more primary documents that alter history's view of the subject, but the original biographer might have had the advantage of interviewing the person's family and friends.

Let's take that hypothetical 1930 medical book as an example. The library has a copy last used in 1952 according to the last stamp on the date due slip. The book was barcoded along with many others in the 1990s when the library staff spent a year barcoding the entire circulating collection in advance of implementing a new integrated library system. The book was sent to storage sometime in the early 2000s and has not been touched since. For many reasons (publication date, obsolescence, no recent circulation activity, shelved in storage) it is an excellent candidate for withdrawal. However, the careful librarian checks local holdings against a large bibliographic utility as one of the steps in processing a long list of potential withdrawal candidates in an automated batch mode. What if this book is the only one in the state or one of only two in the library's primary consortium? What if there are only twelve copies in the country and a total of just nineteen in the world? Even if the bibliographic utility's database undercounts the total because some libraries that hold the title are not members and thus do not list their holdings in it, this is a very low number of copies available worldwide. The book may have no intrinsic value now, and patrons at the local library may never use it again, but the librarian should seriously consider retaining the book as part of the larger obligation to preserve the scholarly record. Perhaps in 2130 a scholar in another state will trace the diagnoses of certain conditions or diseases over the past 300 years, and will borrow this book through interlibrary loan (or, we hope, the copyright laws will have changed enough that by 2130 the 1930 title has made it into the public domain, and that somebody has digitized it in the meantime or can do so on demand when the scholar needs it). The 1930 biography, on the other hand, may also not have interested local patrons for the past several decades, but if there are twenty-two other copies in the state, nine copies in the consortium, and one hundred seventy-nine copies in the country, the library may safely discard its copy. Even when librarians at many other libraries decide to withdraw their copies of the biography, enough of them should keep a copy to provide sufficient access for the foreseeable future.

Of course, the librarian does not make title-by-title decisions about each of these two books. The medical book will drop off the withdrawal candidate list automatically if one of the retention thresholds is set for at least three copies in the consortium; this copy is only one of two of them. The biography will remain on the withdrawal candidate list because there are sufficient other copies available elsewhere. Unless librarians elect to review the lists that meet all the criteria and then mark this title to retain it, the biography will be withdrawn as part of the batch process.

In the past, the major criterion for book withdrawal decisions was local use data. Although this factor plays a role in today's large-scale batch-process book withdrawal projects, it is only one of a large number of factors under consideration.

When Walsh undertook to select books in the classics for storage in the 1950s, he discovered that most of the titles were in effect duplicates (Walsh 1954, 380). The classics primary corpus is static; scholars often tend to use more recent translations, discussions, and printings. The body of work in most other fields is more dynamic. Librarians apply different withdrawal criteria to different subject areas, which are usually identified by their location (e.g., the engineering library, the management library) or by broad call number areas. Ideally, these varying criteria are not too numerous

FIGURE 4.10.

Outline of Book Rightsizing Workflow

Outline of Book Rightsizing Workflow
Determine internal factors for withdrawal criteria.
Prepare catalog extract with internal factors.
Determine external factors for withdrawal criteria.
Run catalog extract against bibliographic utility database to apply external factors (consultant).
Review summary data and adjust parameters until satisfactory.
Prepare final master spreadsheet (pick list), possibly divided into "review" and "no review" lists.
Subdivide list(s) by library location.
Subdivide further if the location lists are very long.
Librarian review (optional).
Delete any titles designated for retention on librarian-reviewed lists.
Send each list to appropriate library location for book withdrawals.
Staff pull books and process them for selected disposal method.
Any books not found are marked in the catalog as missing.
Lists of withdrawn books (minus the missing books) go to technical services.
Technical services staff withdraw the books from the catalog and remove the library's holdings from the bibliographic utility.
Missing books are processed during the next scheduled missing book catalog purge.

or too complicated, or they will render an already-complex process even more difficult to operationalize.

What are the variables for creating the criteria for compiling lists of book withdrawal candidates? There are both internal and external factors to consider. Let's examine the internal ones first.

Internal Factors

Length of Time in the Collection/ Publication Date

The library does not want to withdraw recent publications. What is the cutoff date after which books will automatically remain in the collection? Does this date vary by call number range or by location? One of the project manager's major tasks is to assess colleagues' comfort levels with the local definitions of "low circulation" in relation to the length of time that books have been in the collection. The circulation parameter is usually combined with some kind of time frame. This time frame is determined either by publication date or acquisition date. Libraries generally acquire most books within a year or two of publication, so publication dates are usually good indicators of the length of time that titles have been in the collection. The manager takes into consideration the different "half-life" factors of books in different disciplines. A biology book, for example, may not be very useful after ten years, whereas a mathematics book or a history book may have a much longer potentially useful life. Because it will be confusing to add too many complex date-based formulas, try to limit them to at most two or three, divided by classification ranges or by locations (e.g., the business classification range or the Engineering Library).

Librarians might finally settle on publication date parameters of ten or more years old for science, medical, and technology books and fifteen or more years old for social sciences and humanities titles.

Circulation Activity

Use is still a primary consideration, especially as the initial criterion for determining which titles make it onto the withdrawal candidate list and which do not. A book with zero circulation within the established time frame is easy to understand. But what is "low circulation?" Are two circulations nine years ago for a ten-year-old book equivalent to one circulation one year ago of a twenty-year-old book? What is the right mix of a book's age, the number of circulations, and the date of the circulations to make it a "low-use" book? If browsing figures (books removed from the shelves by users and then noted with a barcode scan before reshelving to capture the use) are included in the ILS, how does this information affect the decision points? The person preparing the lists can provide totals from different scenarios until a number with which the librarians feel comfortable is reached. What happens if a librarian's comfort level is too conservative from the manager's or the administration's perspective? The job then becomes one of assuring colleagues that a slightly higher threshold, although it results in withdrawing more titles, will not impair the collection's usefulness to the user community and, should a withdrawn title later be required, it can easily be borrowed from a partner library or purchased on the used book market.

One point worth mentioning is that querying circulation activity is only useful if the records stretch back a significant number of years. If a library is contemplating implementing a new integrated library system, that planning group should include in the request for proposal (RFP) the requirement that the new system be capable of accepting, merging, and maintaining the previous system's circulation records so that the longevity of the records is maintained. At the author's institution, initial conversations about embarking on a rightsizing project began with the possibility of building a new facility that would contain space for combining several existing libraries, although radically reducing the number of volumes that could be shelved in the new library. The rightsizing project received go-ahead status when the administrators also began planning for a new ILS, and the author pointed out that the library should move with rightsizing as soon as possible to take advantage of the seventeen years of circulation figures in the old system.

"Must-Have" Titles

Some libraries have made blanket decisions that titles that appeared in standard works like *Books for College Libraries* or those reviewed favorably in *Choice* should be retained regardless of past local use patterns. Librarians should consider this approach carefully. What is the value of retaining "good" books that nobody reads?

Language

How do foreign-language titles fit into the mix? Many libraries find that these books are consistently low-use titles. It may help to evaluate the institution's current foreign-language programs. If Russian is no longer being taught, for example, most books in that language might be withdrawal candidates. It may be useful to keep some books on learning various languages whereas, for example, a 1975 book in Portuguese on politics in Mozambique may now be of very limited value. Be aware, however, that some titles, although unused locally, may be relatively scarce; if so, librarians should seriously consider keeping them for the good of the scholarly community at large.

Local Publications

The library should maintain as complete a collection as possible of its own institution's publications. Librarians also decide how heavily to invest in retaining widely held publications about the local city, state, or region.

Collections of Distinction

Are there some subject areas for which the library should keep most material regardless of its age or utility to the local user community? For some libraries, the answer is yes. If some of the institution's programs are regionally, nationally, or internationally renowned, the library may want to maintain print collections representing that subject's full historical breadth and depth, even if some of the titles would otherwise have met withdrawal criteria. The subject may be as broad as a complete discipline, such as aeronautical engineering, or it might be fairly narrow, such as apiculture, primatology, or turf grass management. Not all the material need be kept in the active collection; some may be removed to a storage facility, if available, and some may be candidates for inclusion in the special collections department. One author's term for material like this was *working heritage collection* (McCarthy 2007, 348).

Curriculum

Did the institution recently close a department or program? If so, many of the specialized but widely held works on those areas may be candidates for withdrawal.

Location or Status

Librarians identify groups of books to exclude from consideration, such as titles in special collections or on reserve or reference. Government publications may form another exclusion. Any books flagged as missing or lost should be excluded too. If the storage facility will not be part of the rightsizing project, then that location should be excluded. Titles currently in circulation can be excluded. If there are special shelf location codes for the storage facility, librarians should note which additional fields must be included in the storage lists.

Format

Mixing formats on the same candidate list can be confusing. Save microform and audiovisual material for separate lists, and exclude other formats, such as maps. Remember to exclude electronic books.

Key Words

Are there some distinctive key words that should trigger exclusions, such as the name of the institution and any other names or words with special local significance?

■ ■ ■

An expert can filter in or out the preceding factors while creating a query to run against the library's ILS. The manager will indicate which record fields should appear on the output, including any special field for storage shelf location numbers if pertinent. The result will be the first iteration of the withdrawal candidate pool. The manager or other team members should review and sample this first list. Are there still classes of items on the list that should have been excluded? If so, sort and delete them or ask for a second run that accounts for the new variable.

Many libraries have conducted successful projects using only internal factors to develop their withdrawal candidate lists. Until fairly recently, it was not possible to apply further filters, especially in a large-scale automated way. Now it is possible to apply other criteria to withdrawal candidate lists to shape better decisions at the local level while considering factors on a much broader scale. In general, these additional factors require matching the local list against the much larger database provided by the bibliographic utility that the library uses. Such matching is currently best accomplished by employing the services of a consultant with a relationship with the bibliographic utility. The consultant will start with the catalog extract that the library prepared based on internal criteria, and then apply the external criteria after running the extract against the bibliographic utility's database. However, even using a consultant, it is the librarians' job to set the various thresholds for a number of external factors.

External factors

Regional Considerations

A library, especially if it is state-supported, may want to be sure that it retains the last copy of any title held in its local state or region. If a library has the only major collection in a certain subject area in its state or region, administrators should consider maintaining it as a regional resource even if parts of it are no longer important to the local user community. Libraries in state-supported institutions may feel a greater imperative to do this than those in private institutions. Examples might be a library supporting the only dental school or veterinary medicine school in the state. A small- or medium-sized library might want to confirm that the state's largest academic library holds a copy of the material before withdrawing its own.

Consortial Holdings

Even if a library is conducting a rightsizing project on its own, it should compare withdrawal candidates against the holdings of its consortial partners. How many copies should be available in the consortium before librarians feel comfortable withdrawing their own? This can be a tricky question, since there is no assurance that the other libraries will keep their copies. If four other libraries hold a title today, for example, two or three of them might withdraw their copies over the next few years. Librarians hope that their colleagues at those institutions will also check consortial holdings during their own rightsizing efforts, and will also make withdrawal decisions that leave at least two copies in the consortium.

"Keeper" Libraries

Some of the larger research libraries have informal reputations as "keeper" libraries. They often support enormous storage facilities from which it is unlikely that they will discard much, if anything. The rightsizing library may be able to identify several of these libraries within its consortium, plus a group of fifty to a hundred geographically dispersed libraries and determine how many copies must also be held among them before it will discard its own. It is always a bit of a gamble to assume that these large libraries are likely to retain most of their books, so librarians also should check that sufficient copies remain in the region or country.

Wider Holdings

Beyond consortial holdings, how many other copies exist in the region or country? What is the total number of holdings below which librarians feel an obligation to keep their library's copy for the good of the whole? A rule of thumb in the United States might be to retain a book locally if national holdings total thirty or fewer copies. If at some future point it is easy to tell, for example, that twelve of those thirty copies already reside in collaborative print retention facilities, then librarians might feel comfortable withdrawing a local instance of a relatively scarce copy.

Figure 4.11 lists titles that appeared on the author's institution's final book withdrawal candidate list, along with the number of copies held elsewhere in the United States at the time.

After establishing these multiple thresholds, it is natural to wonder if any titles at all will be left as withdrawal candidates, but even with all these exclusions and stipulations, tens or hundreds of thousands of book titles will remain that match all the criteria. If the library hired a consultant to prepare the list, she typically prepares a summary showing how many titles will be on the final pick list given different values for selected thresholds. For example, if the resulting number of titles in the pool seems low and if the librarians had suggested the availability of at least five other copies in their primary consortium before their copy appeared on the withdrawal candidate list, the consultant may recommend running the numbers again with the parameter of at least two or three other copies in the consortium.

When everyone agrees on the final numbers for each criterion, the consultant will conduct the final compilation and deliver the final spreadsheet (i.e., the pick list). The spreadsheet contains all the information needed to make final retention decisions, to find and remove items, and to update catalog records. In addition to the standard bibliographic information, the final list will show parameters such as the number of uses and browses, the number of other holding libraries in various categories, and local information such as location, call number, and barcode.

It may be useful to divide the final results into two main categories. One is a *no review list* containing the titles of books with no uses (and perhaps only one use) during the period under consideration (typically the activation date of the last ILS through the cutoff date selected for list generation). The second is a *review list* for books with, perhaps, two or three uses during the same

FIGURE 4.11.

Examples of Low- and No-Use Book Titles

Title	Imprint	US Holdings
The financial interdependence of the economy, 1957-1966 [by Alan R. Roe]	Cambridge, Chapman & Hall, 1971.	53
The workshop of the world; British economic history from 1820 to 1880.	London, New York, Oxford University Press, 1961.	200
The logic of British and American industry; a realistic analysis of economic structure and government.	Chapel Hill, University of North Carolina Press [1953]	167
Industrial reconstruction and the control of competition; the British experiments, by Arthur Fletcher Lucas.	London, New York [etc.] Longmans, Green and Co. [1937]	150
Economy and society in nineteenth-century Britain [by] Richard Tames.	London, Allen & Unwin [1972]	107
Bloodless invasion; German economic penetration into Danubian states and the Balkans, by Paul Einzig.	London, Duckworth [1938]	75
The Austrian economy since 1945.	London, New York, Royal Institute of International Affairs [1950]	96
Mouvement économique en France de 1944 à 1957.	Paris, Impr. nationale, 1958.	54
Industries of Norway; technical and commercial achievements.	[Oslo] Dreyer [c1952]	116
Economic policy in practice; the Netherlands 1950/1957.	Leiden, H. E. Stenfert Kroese, 1959.	97
The economic history of Korea, from the earliest times to 1945, by Hochin Choi.	Seoul, Freedom Library [1971]	65
The Imperial impact : studies in the economic history of Africa and India / edited by Clive Dewey and A.G. Hopkins.	London : Athlone Press for the Institute of Commonwealth Studies, 1978.	169
India / by Jagdish N. Bhagwati, T. N. Srinivasan.	New York : National Bureau of Economic Research : distributed by Columbia University Press, 1975.	200
Introduction to labor economics.	New York, McGraw-Hill, 1955.	117

period. The titles on the no review list will have had such minimal use that librarians can probably withdraw them without qualms; however, they may want to glance at the review list in case there are a few titles that, despite low use and wide availability elsewhere, the library should retain.

It is then the manager's task to take the master spreadsheet and break it into manageable sublists, for example, Main, Science, Art, Engineering, and

Storage. If there are both review and no review master lists, then designate the sublists as Main1 (review), Main2 (no review), Sci1, Sci2, and so on. If some of these sublists are still extremely long, it will be helpful to divide them further, such as Main1A, Main1B, Main1C, and so forth. A good rule of thumb is that a book review list should be no more than about 3,000 lines. Staff will feel overwhelmed if presented with a list of several tens of thousands of titles for review or pulling.

Thus the file named `Storage2A` (the first review list for Storage) might have 3,000 titles in the call number range for history. The history librarian reviews it, and marks, for example, 264 titles to retain, possibly by making Xs in a new column labeled "Mark X to Retain." The manager then saves the file as `Storage2Arev` (the addition of "rev" to the file name indicates it has been reviewed) and deletes the retention titles as indicated. If the storage location has special shelf location codes, the manager sorts the list in order by the codes before sending it. In a manner similar to managing the journal lists and sublists, the manager maintains a log showing the various stages through which each list travels.

The staff that pull the books should mark the lists to show which titles were removed and which were not found. They should also make any other notes for situations that a supervisor will need to resolve, such as finding a multivolume set for which only some of the volumes are designated for withdrawal. Books found to be checked out to users should be removed from the list; this indication of current use suggests that the title should remain in the library. Any books that are missing from the stacks should be marked as missing in the ILS so that they will be formally searched again during the library's next routine missing book review process. If they later resurface, the staff will see a note to withdraw them. If they are still not located at that time, they will be withdrawn. After processing, the supervisor removes from the list any titles that were not found and forwards the spreadsheet, now showing only those titles that were withdrawn, to technical services. Staff in technical services complete the process of withdrawing the titles from the catalog and removing the library's holdings from the bibliographic utility's database. Using the books' standard numbers as they appear on the list, these withdrawals occur in batch mode.

The reader may note that this book recommends having journal records updated to withdrawn *before* the volumes are pulled, yet recommends having book records updated to withdrawn *after* the titles are pulled. For journals, it is better to update the catalog before pulling the volumes so that staff can identify and solve in advance small problems like, for example, the first volume after a title change bound together with the last volume from the previous title. If a journal volume is missing when staff pull volumes, it will not matter because the whole run is being withdrawn anyway. For books, missing titles or other problems should be noted before the catalog records are updated to withdrawn. However, although updating journal catalog records before withdrawal is ideal, librarians responding to a tight deadline to remove material to make space before a construction project may have to pull first and update later.

MANAGING WORKFLOW:
MICROFORM AND AUDIOVISUAL MATERIAL

It should be possible to generate lists of items in nonprint formats from the ILS, possibly by location and by format. To avoid confusion, it may be advisable to work with one format at a time, or with one location at a time. Figure 4.12 shows part of a withdrawal candidate list of microform titles compiled from an ILS. An actual list would include bibliographic utility numbers so that technical services staff could withdraw titles from both the ILS and from the bibliographic utility in a batch process. Most microform will not have circulation figures, so if librarians review the candidate lists, they will make retention decisions based on the titles and their relevance to the current curriculum.

The general caveat for these formats is to be aware that some of the items in the library's collection might have been issued as United States *government documents* as part of the federal document depository program, in which case it is important to follow federal guidelines for withdrawal. Try to exclude government documents from lists generated from the library's ILS or, if this is either impossible or only partially successful, search the resulting spreadsheets before further processing and delete any government documents. (Should the library wish to implement a government documents rightsizing plan, this project will require frequent input from the government documents librarian and general awareness of the multiple types and formats involved: serials, monographs, print, microform, CD-ROM, and so forth.)

Technical reports deserve special mention. Many academic libraries have significant collections of these reports, especially in areas of engineering, technology, and science. Some are cataloged as serials, some as monographs. It is also likely that many of these will not be cataloged or barcoded or, if cataloged, will include hundreds or thousands of reports under a monographic serial title. Many items may also be federal government publications, although not all of them will have been acquired through the federal depository program. The result is a large collection of low-use material for which there are few, if any, circulation records. Complications may arise because many of these reports may be on microform and, because these are titles that other holding libraries also have not cataloged or have cataloged as monographic serials, a dilemma arises about what to do with them as withdrawal candidates. Many of them may now be available in digital versions; it might be feasible to discard

FIGURE 4.12.

Sample Microform Withdrawal Candidate List

Call Number	Author	Title	Imprint
297.870924 X105B Un3		*Malcolm X [microform] : FBI surveillance file.*	Scholarly Resources,
301.4522 C437w	Child, Lydia Maria	*Works of Lydia Maria Francis Child [microform]*	3M International Microfilm Press,
322.440973 B561		*Black Abolitionist papers, 1830-1865 [microform].*	Microfilming Corporation of America,
323.40924 K585Z Un3		*Martin Luther King, Jr. FBI assassination file*	Scholarly Resources,
325.31410973 R245		*Records of the British Colonial Office, class 5*	University Publications of America,
325.342 G798a	Great Britain. Colonial Office.	*Annual reports on the colonies [microform]*	Andronicus Pub. Co.,
327.41 C76 1985		*Confidential U.S. State Department central files.*	University Publications of America,
362.0924 Ad21B	Addams, Jane	*Letters and related papers in the following collections*	Yale University Library,
362.0924 Ad21Z B84		*Jane Addams papers [microform]*	University Microfilms International,
363.2820973 L5695		*Letters received by the Attorney General, 1809-1870*	University Publications of America,
808.2 C838		*Covent Garden prompt books [microform].*	Micro Photo Division, Bell & Howell,
811 W61x	Whittier, John Greenleaf	*Works of John G. Whittier [microform]*	3M International Microfilm Press,
818 C362x	Channing, William Ellery	*Works of William E. Channing [microform].*	J. Munroe,
917.504 OL5w	Olmsted, Frederick Law	*Works of Frederick Law Olmsted [microform]*	3M International Microfilm Press,
943.087 G317r		*Reports of the military government for Germany*	Scholarly Resources Inc.,
943.6052 Au79r		*Reports of the U.S. military government of Austria*	Scholarly Resources Inc.,
970.00497 R245 1993		*Records of the American Indian Institute [microform]*	Presbyterian Historical Society,
970.1 Am354		*American Indian correspondence : [microform]*	Greenwood Press,
970.108 Se48 1977		*Selected works by American Indian authors*	New York Public Library,
973.0496073 C76c		*Congress of Racial Equality (CORE) papers*	University Publications of America,
973.0992 Am35 1989		*American immigrant autobiographies [microform].*	University Publications of America,
973.3 J331c	Jay, John	*Correspondence and public papers of John Jay*	Putnam,
973.917 M823p	Morgenthau, Henry	*Presidential diaries of Henry Morgenthau, Jr.*	University Publications of America,

the print in those cases, although such a project might involve checking thousands of titles. In the case of the monographic serial titles, many individual reports may be bound into a single volume, and in some cases only some of the reports in the volume might have been digitized. Low-use technical reports could be prime candidates for a collaborative storage venture, although the fact that so many of them are uncataloged may be a stumbling block. Lucker and his colleagues suggested identifying essential series to keep in full and, for the rest, keeping a certain number of recent years. Exceptions would be foreign technical reports, which are more difficult to obtain quickly if needed (Lucker, Herzog, and Owens 1986, 21).

Some large *microform* sets are now available in digital form. Libraries that buy the electronic versions can discard their microform; there is very little interest in this format. Even smaller institutions that do not have this content in either format will probably decline even a gift of the microform sets.

Bear in mind that some microform may not have been cataloged. For example, engineering libraries do not catalog the tens of thousands of microfiche reports obtained from the National Technical Information Service (NTIS); these are filed in cabinets by report number.

Librarians should consider retaining some microform titles even if they are duplicated by print or online equivalents. Examples would be the campus and local newspapers.

Does the library still house stand-alone *CD-ROMs* (that is, those that were not issued as supplements with print books)? If so, have they been used recently? In all likelihood, most of any remaining stand-alone CD-ROMs are outdated and can be withdrawn *en masse*. Be aware, however, that some CD-ROMs may have been purchased from publishers with specific conditions about the ultimate disposal of the disks; others may contain sensitive information. Although the likelihood of nefarious use being made of discarded CD-ROMs is low, it would be advisable to dispose of them in such a way that no further use can be made of them. Sands described nearly a dozen options for destroying CD-ROMs (Sands 1991).

Although there is no longer much demand for this format, the library may have a collection of *VHS tapes* that the publishers have not reissued in newer formats and that some professors still like to use in class. After double-checking for DVD, Blu-ray, or streaming availability, librarians can try to get the publisher's written permission to copy the VHS tape onto a DVD and then archive or discard the VHS version. Consultation with professors may identify acceptable alternatives in DVD format. Frequently used tapes may simply disintegrate; withdraw them if they are no longer playable. One advantage of retiring all VHS tapes is that the equipment needed to view them can then also be discarded.

Periodic review of *DVD or Blu-ray* titles is just as important as reviewing the print book collection. Some may be damaged. A part of a multidisc set may be missing, in which case the librarian decides whether to replace the set entirely or withdraw it. Some may be outdated, just as books can be, and thus candidates for withdrawal. Others may simply not have received enough use to justify keeping them. Librarians should be aware of the reasons for buying some of the titles in the first place. If, for example, the institution has a film department, and the library specifically added DVDs of all movies that won a Best Picture Academy Award, the library should keep *The Life of Emile Zola* (1937) even if it is not a high-use title. Some libraries supplement their DVD/Blu-ray collection with subscriptions to services that provide streaming content. Over time, these subscriptions, or a combination of subscriptions to a variety of services, may eliminate the need to build and maintain a DVD/Blu-ray collection.

LPs, audio tapes, and *cassettes* may be of greatest interest to libraries in institutions with music programs. Most music libraries now subscribe to services that provide their students with access to music performances, but it may be important to keep a few of these older formats if, for example, there is no online equivalent for certain pieces, or if an instructor wants to keep a recording of a particular artist's performance. However, libraries with a collection of these items acquired for general use may wish to withdraw them, along with any equipment needed to play them, if use no longer justifies their retention.

Other Material

Libraries contain other material that they may want to consider withdrawing. *Maps* are one example. Librarians with experience rightsizing books and journals can adapt the processes they have developed and apply them to other material.

RAPID-RESPONSE SCENARIO

The literature reports more and more instances of libraries facing unexpected situations in which they must suddenly reduce their footprint. Looming remodeling or construction deadlines mandate that certain areas be cleared. Rampant mold or a leaky ceiling require immediate removal of affected material. The university administration unexpectedly designates a certain area of library space to be transformed for nonlibrary services and functions. An entire floor may be slated for reflooring. Suddenly, the library finds itself in crisis mode to accommodate the deadline. Under such circumstances, staff may initially grapple with fear and panic, and then pull together to make the best of these situations—"making lemonade from lemons" as one article expressed it (Tobia and Feldman, 2010). These situations almost invariably require reducing the size of the physical collection, often on a very tight schedule. The earlier librarians learn about the impending change, the sooner they can become part of the solution.

These situations often allow little time for thoughtful evaluation of that part of the collection that is under siege; under pressure, the easiest solution usually seems to be moving everything somewhere else as soon as possible to free up the affected area. Still, in all but the most urgent cases, it is possible to view the deadline-driven situation as an opportunity to conduct at least some weeding activities first and thus move a selected portion rather than the whole collection.

Let's examine a case study from the author's experience. At her institution, the audiovisual (A/V) collection was located in the Undergraduate Library. There was a moderate-sized microform collection in the adjacent Humanities, Social Sciences, and Education (HSSE) Library. The library had scheduled a large traveling exhibit with a fixed and advertised arrival date for the Undergraduate Library. The exhibit was due to arrive in three weeks. The best place to set up this display was in the area occupied by the A/V shelves. The administrators decided to move the A/V collection permanently to the HSSE Library next to the microform collection, but the only way that it would fit would be to remove some of the microform cabinets before moving and then reassembling the A/V shelves. One approach would have been simply to move several rows of full microform cabinets to the library's local storage facility and thus make room for the A/V shelves. However, microform is a very low-use collection. Although the tight schedule was not ideal, pulling together to make the effort to identify titles to withdraw would accomplish two goals: permanently reduce the footprint of seldom-used material and free up the space needed for the A/V collection.

The author had some months previously requested and received a detailed Excel spreadsheet of all the HSSE microform titles. She quickly divided the master spreadsheet into several shorter lists: government publications, serials, monographs, and reference. She posted the first three lists to a shared drive and asked HSSE subject specialists to review the lists very quickly and mark any titles that should be retained. They responded promptly; ten days before the deadline, support staff took the lists and began to withdraw titles that had not been marked for retention. Staff moved the weeded microform onto carts to free up space as quickly as possible; final disposition was handled after the deadline. Enough material was removed so that staff could then shift the remaining microform into the first few rows of cabinets. The last rows of now-empty cabinets were then removed, leaving space for the A/V shelving. A few cabinets were moved to a short-term holding area so that HSSE librarians could later review some material that they wanted to examine more closely before making retention decisions; the material that they decided to keep from these cabinets was relocated to the storage facility. The spreadsheets contained enough information for technical services staff to make changes to both the local catalog and to the bibliographic utility some weeks after the wild weeding and relocation project. Because all the A/V titles had simply moved from one place to another, catalog updates for them only involved a global location change. Fortunately, staff had recently weeded the A/V collection, so there was no need to try and review those titles as well.

Obviously, it is not ideal to handle a relocation project by dropping almost everything else to rush to meet a deadline. However, it can be done, and in many cases it can be combined with at least some weeding activity to remove titles that no longer need to be kept. However, such a project requires designating someone to direct the activity and to coordinate and inform staff in multiple areas. In the case study above, the author kept in close contact with employees in multiple locations: the Undergraduate Library, the HSSE Library, technical services, the administration, the storage facility, and the department that handles physically moving items throughout the library system.

This example described a small project with a deadline only a few weeks away. Some librarians find themselves facing massive reduction projects on short notice. If the impetus for the project comes from the central university administration, these administrators are usually willing to offer some compensation in return for the lost library space. Many libraries have received one-time special funding to purchase journal backfiles so that the equivalent print volumes can be withdrawn without loss of content. The university may pay for compact or other new shelving, temporary staff, a consultant, or other costs associated with moving or removing material. The library administrators can negotiate for anything from cosmetic enhancements (e.g., new furniture, carpet, or paint) to major overhauls that involve creating features such as an information commons or new study rooms.

Faced with a tight deadline, administrators must identify key players for the team that will manage the project and draw up an action plan. As far as collections are concerned, the questions revolve around what to keep, what to store, and what to withdraw. For many libraries, the storage variable is not an option so the project boils down to what material must be withdrawn to meet the goal of freeing up the required space.

The most obvious—and generally the largest— part of the solution usually focuses on reducing the size of a print journal collection as the means of creating the greatest amount of space in the shortest period of time. If the library has already purchased perpetual access e-journals, the project manager can begin almost immediately by identifying these titles. With a limited time frame, it may not be possible to include a review process, or the review process must be accelerated. It may be necessary to take the shortcut of moving or removing material quickly, and then catching up with updating records later. Clear and updated signage helps users find items during the transition.

If there is an area of the library that can tolerate the load, if funds are available for purchase, and if space can be reconfigured around it, then compact shelving may solve part of the problem. One library put books that had not circulated within the past decade and that were also older than a particular date into compact shelving. A combination of withdrawals and shifting into areas formerly occupied by the books could then accommodate the remaining print journal collection (Tooey 2010, 41).

In the end, the authors of most "how we survived" articles agreed that after getting past the initial shock, staff realized that the enforced change gave the library a new kind of opportunity to support the institution's educational mission and offered some benefits that would not otherwise have been possible. The changes helped staff realize "that the library was more than its collections" (Thibodeau 2010, 28). Mandated reductions of physical collections force librarians to think creatively about offering new or different services. Many authors commented on the positive effects of adjacent unrelated offices, classrooms, or services; these new areas attracted people who, after conducting their business there, stayed in the library to study and use the library's resources. These projects often resulted in renovations that the library could not have afforded; for example, Haynes appreciated the "more modern, updated look and feel for the library" (Haynes 2010, 34).

As with the end of a planned rightsizing project, at the end of a mandated renovation and repurposing project it will be tempting to sit back and recover from the stress of these fast-paced and at least initially unwelcome changes. A better plan would be to channel the momentum of the work into an ongoing effort to continue identifying and withdrawing physical material that no longer serves the user community well. Freiburger remarked that following a sudden downsizing effort to accommodate loss of space, "the library is now in a state of continuous weeding" in part to provide more study space and to alleviate crowded shelves, and in part in anticipation of future outside demands on library space (Freiburger 2010, 31).

The reality is that most libraries do not need as much space for collections as they did in the past. "Continuing pressures on library space are inevitable. . . . Libraries must have a compelling vision, strong campus advocates, and data to justify space allocation as more and more information is digital" (Persily and Butter 2010, 47). The emphasis is rapidly shifting to electronic collections and to improved study and learning spaces, as well as to the services that support changing user needs. One library reported proactively offering space to its campus, which was experiencing critical space needs, and thus created "an opportunity to articulate needs and, as part of a renovation, reenvision certain areas of the library" (Tooey 2010, 41). These librarians became *partners* in space reallocation, not self-perceived victims. This inspiring tale suggests that library administrators could consider drawing up realistic space allocation plans and revising them periodically as rightsizing and other activities change the shape and use of library areas. The call may never come, but if it does, librarians will be far better prepared to act in a positive and proactive manner that will benefit their users, their institution, and themselves.

It is worth mentioning that some rapid-response scenarios come about by welcome opportunities rather than by external pressures. The literature reports several withdrawal projects undertaken when a library received funding for a needed renovation or beneficial space reorganization (Crosetto, Kinner, and Duhon 2008; Gallagher and Rathemacher 2012).

"Rapid" is also a relative term. Depending on the size of the library and the scale of the rightsizing project, having only two or three years for a comprehensive review of the collection and completion of the deselection process before the beginning of a construction project or a move into a new building may require working at a breathless pace.

PROJECT CONCLUSION

When the last book comes off the shelves or the last empty microform cabinet is wheeled away, there is a good reason both to celebrate its conclusion and to document the project's success.

Celebration

When the retrospective portion of the rightsizing project ends, the administration should coordinate (and fund) a celebratory event. This not only acknowledges the work of the staff who participated in various aspects of the project, but also demonstrates the administration's commitment to the need for rightsizing the library's physical collection and the achievement of an important strategic goal. The rightsizing project may well have been one of the largest projects that the library has ever undertaken. In one way or another it will have touched nearly every unit. Its conclusion is a reason for the whole system to celebrate, not just the staff who were most closely involved in its implementation.

Project Assessment

The project manager should write a report for the administrators. The report will document the criteria used and provide a brief description of the workflow. It should include any statistics about the project, suggest changes for future efforts, and recommend a plan for undertaking ongoing routine and periodic collection evaluation. The report will also acknowledge the work undertaken by staff in multiple units who contributed to the project's success. It should also document any unexpected outcomes, such as the benefit of improving camaraderie and communication between staff members who ordinarily do not work much together or the ability to recognize gaps in the collection, or the fact that "weeding is no longer the dreaded task it used to be" (Soma and Sjoberg 2011, 25–26). One librarian reported that collaborating with faculty during a weeding project improved communication and "positioned the librarians as colleagues to the teaching faculty for consultations in other areas, such as the support for the development of effective research assignments" (Dubicki 2008, 135).

Plan Routine Rightsizing

Library administrators are responsible for developing plans for ongoing routine collection assessment. These might include handling journal lists at the time that the library acquires new perpetual access packages, marking calendars to review the JSTOR list every three years, or withdrawing reference sets when their electronic equivalents become available. It is important to assign responsibility to the staff who should handle these ongoing tasks. Monograph reviews might occur once a decade; material that was relatively active ten years ago might have entered its period of declining use by then. Administrators set an anticipated time line for future work and assign someone to remind key players or their successors when review dates arrive.

Continuous Assessment

Whether a rightsizing project begins in response to a sudden or planned need to reduce the physical collection's footprint, there is a natural tendency to ramp up for large-scale work to meet deadlines and then to relax when those deadlines are met. Letting a rightsizing project fizzle out when the immediate crisis is past does not capitalize on the the resources and processes that are already in place, making it easy to continue or expand the project even if the pace slows. If the periodical stacks have been substantially reduced to make way for renovated study space, for example, attention can turn to a more leisurely examination of the book collection or the contents of the microform cabinets. Even if the library has met the goal of removing a target amount of material, there may still be additional titles that meet the withdrawal criteria. When the library buys the next journal backfile, for instance, it makes sense to review it soon after acquisition to identify the equivalent print that may no longer be needed. A thorough rightsizing project completed last year will have identified medium-use titles many of which will, over the following decade or two, become low-use titles. The library administration must decide whether to continue rightsizing activities in at least a small way, or whether to declare a project finished and then revive it some years later when the need arises again.

Assessment does not just occur at the end of a project. Plans and procedures that looked good at the beginning of a project may, after some experience with them, benefit from some process improvement. For example, one college library embarked on a comprehensive weeding plan expected to take between eight and twelve years to complete because of the careful evaluation that the librarians planned to do. After some experience with the plan, librarians devised a number of smaller special projects for "materials that could be evaluated and removed quickly and easily from the collection . . . [to] improve the quality of the collection and ease congestion in the stacks." One of the special projects involved weeding the crowded shelves containing computer manuals, many of which were outdated and unused. Another project involved weeding books from a series now available online (Soma and Sjoberg 2011, 23).

5

The Future of Physical Collections in Academic Libraries

ALTHOUGH PREDICTIONS CAN BE TRICKY, LET'S LOOK AT SOME likely future trends for physical collections in academic libraries.

LOCAL COLLECTIONS

Most long-established college and university libraries are likely to maintain a circulating collection of physical material for some time. Even after a large rightsizing project, many titles that remain in print or in other physical form will continue to meet the current needs of students and researchers. In many libraries, this material will now form a true core collection. For some time in the future, many books will continue to be issued exclusively in print, or be issued in print many months before the electronic versions appear, so libraries will continue to buy selected titles in print. Wholesale digitization with full-text availability of the enormous post-1922 corpus is unlikely for both economic and legal reasons, so libraries will continue to maintain these books, although fewer copies will be collectively retained. Individual libraries will undertake to keep various no- or low-use physical items that are scarce or that cover topics of local interest, or because the library agreed to be the consortial or regional holder for certain titles. Librarians will be more apt to identify as many as half a dozen collections of distinction in subject areas for which their institution is particularly renowned, and maintain larger physical collections in those areas, even if some of them are not heavily used. Archives and special collections will continue to gain in importance, and libraries will invest in more space for them, particularly the kind of specialized space needed to hold and preserve rare and fragile items, including nonprint material like memorabilia.

The collection on the far side of a major rightsizing project will be more clearly focused on the user community's current needs. As publishers issue more and more of their content electronically, as libraries acquire more and more of that content on an electronic-preferred basis, and as users become more and more comfortable with using that format, the rate of acquiring physical information objects will decline.

Most academic librarians will find it beneficial to start consciously moving away from the traditional just-in-case model of collection development and embrace just-in-time models. Patron-driven acquisitions plans meet this need to a significant degree. By waiting until a patron expresses a need for a book and then acquiring it rapidly (interlibrary loan book purchase programs) or seamlessly (e-book PDA plans), librarians accomplish several things. First, they conserve funds by paying only for what their patrons use. Second, patron-selected books have a high likelihood of greater future use. These just-in-time acquisition plans should not, of course, completely replace librarian selections. Negotiating "big deals" to buy important publishers' outputs at a low per-unit cost is one example of librarians' continuing role in collection development. Another example is buying specialized material, such as scientific conference proceeding or foreign language titles, that is unlikely to be available in PDA plans in the near future. Over time it will be necessary to review the group of PDA titles and remove older, unused ones to keep the selection current and relevant.

In conjunction with these practices, librarians should reassess their approval plans. Using plans that pour more print titles, or even electronic ones, into a library just because they meet a subject profile or are part of the annual output of a certain publisher is not necessarily the best way to continue building most collections. Perpetuating traditional collection development models simply by moving from print books on shelves to electronic books in cyberspace also perpetuates the problems we have examined in this book, that of obscuring useful titles by surrounding them with hundreds that patrons find less useful. It is time to rethink how and when libraries acquire titles. Owning tens of thousands of unused e-books is no better than owning their unused print counterparts, especially when in so many cases it is both easy and cost effective to add the records for many of these titles into a catalog or discovery layer and wait for patron use to drive acquisition.

REGIONAL AND RESEARCH MEGA-COLLECTIONS

There are several types of academic libraries for which rightsizing is not appropriate, because they serve as the "keeper" libraries for everyone else. One type comprises the libraries at top research institutions, with holdings of millions of volumes, many of which are kept in their own storage facilities or in facilities jointly maintained with several peer institutions. Another type is national libraries; some are considered libraries of last resort for resource sharing, and others collect comprehensively in part to support the research needs of their constituents. A third type is the consortial collection, held either centrally or in a distributed arrangement, in which millions of volumes are held as part of last-copy agreements mainly for members of the participating group, but usually including resource sharing privileges for others. The fourth type may be a relatively small and specialized library holding largely unique collections in its niche area, such as at a nationally renowned botanical garden, zoo, or museum. These libraries will not undertake rightsizing projects because their missions require them to build, retain, and maintain comprehensive collections. These are the collections upon which other libraries may depend, at least in part, when making their own withdrawal decisions.

There are two important points to consider about keeper libraries. First, they have made enormous and ongoing commitments in terms of money, staff, facilities, and preservation. Although they maintain these collections primarily for their own users or for contributing consortial members, most of the items in these collections are available to others through interlibrary loan. In recognition of the commitments that these keeper libraries have undertaken, nonaffiliated libraries that borrow from them should willingly pay premium fees on those relatively few occasions that they must borrow scarce items, or items that the facility maintains so that dozens of other libraries can discard their own low-use copies. Paying that occasional one-time expensive loan fee may in fact be almost a benefit for the borrowing library that did not itself have to maintain a copy of the item locally for a much higher cumulative ongoing cost over the next hundred years, because it could rely on the keeper library to supply it when needed.

Second, a local rightsizing project does not imply that a library will withdraw all its low- and no-use titles and thereafter rely totally and exclusively on other collections to lend obscure items. Librarians who undertake rightsizing projects should ensure that part of the process involves capturing information about the relative scarcity of the titles eligible for withdrawal. Each library should be willing to retain material that is not widely held, no matter how irrelevant is has become for the local user population, in the interests of preserving an adequate number of copies of scholarly works for the good of the larger community. For most libraries, there will not be a large percentage of items that fall into this category, but it is important to make a conscious effort to keep it and to share it when requested.

Demas and Lougee wrote about collective action as a strategy and called for "even more radical collaboration among libraries." They envisioned the combination of shared print archiving and shared digital archiving, thus providing a future in which there is widespread access to digital copies combined with "cooperative retention of print versions as back-up" that will reduce collection redundancies and "create economies of scale that benefit individual institutions and the community as a whole." They expressed concern about the fact that it is "unclear how these independent efforts will be effectively knit into a coordinated national program" in the United States because, unlike plans in some other countries, the collective archiving effort is not being led or directed by a national entity, but rather by a number of different groups each focused mainly on its own members (Demas and Lougee 2011, 2–3). Initiatives such as the Print Archive and Preservation Registry (PAPR), which lists journal runs archived as part of various consortial collaborative projects, are promising developments towards at least a national network.

CHANGING PUBLISHING MODELS

The next revolution in scholarly publishing may involve new models for journal articles. Users may be becoming less concerned about where a particular article appears than in the fact that the article meets their needs. Although they may not articulate it, academic library users are increasingly more interested in instant access at the article level than at the journal level. New models may emerge in which libraries provide access to articles in much the same way that they currently do for books in the PDA model: rather than buying subscriptions to thousands of journal titles, they will load millions of profiled article records into the discovery layer and pay for them when their patrons use them.

In short, most academic libraries will acquire material that meets their users' immediate needs, usually in electronic format and often using various just-in-time acquisition models linked to patron-driven selection methods. Libraries will maintain and preserve unique, rare, and scarce material, and will be active participants in local, regional, and consortial collaborative efforts to store and maintain a limited number of copies of low-use physical items for the collective good.

A few academic libraries will stand apart from many of these general trends. For example, libraries on new campuses will open with heavily electronic retrospective collections and then continue to buy largely electronic resources whenever possible. Print and other physical material will play a very small role in these libraries.

One concern that some librarians raise about this new vision of the academic library is the fear that by embracing new collection development models such as buying books and journals in packages, only keeping higher use titles, and relying more on patron-driven acquisitions, many library collections will become cookie-cutter copies of each other. Because colleges and universities offer diverse programs and their faculty engage in a wide variety of research activities, the goal is that each institution will acquire the titles that best match the needs of its users. Having said that, many institutions do offer programs or undertake research agendas that are similar to those elsewhere, especially at the undergraduate level. In the new model, some titles will still be heavily used at many libraries and the core collection may look somewhat alike at similar kinds of institutions that offer the same kinds of programs. Is this a bad outcome if the patrons use some of the same titles at dozens or hundreds of libraries? If librarians are buying the right material, or offering records of the right material from which their patrons can select, then everyone is happy: users, librarians, vendors, and publishers alike.

What if hardly anyone selects some titles in a publishers' offerings? If no one uses certain titles in PDA plans, then libraries do not pay for them, and vendors and publishers receive no revenue for these items. This is a tough question. In the past, publishers could rely on at least a few hundred sales from research libraries for even the most obscure publication. In the new environment, most librarians will decline to buy these titles outright, having learned from past experience that patron use will probably be very low to nonexistent. At most, they may add these types of titles to their patron-driven acquisition lists, but if few patrons use them, then there will be few sales. Over time, publishers may become more reluctant to produce and offer titles in areas of very narrow interest in esoteric subjects. Does this mean that future or emerging areas of scholarship will never see the light of cultural immortality in the written (or digital) word? It seems likely that many of these works' authors will find alternative ways to express them. Formal publishing is no longer the only or the major avenue for scholarly communication and forward-thinking librarians are actively exploring ways to capture, describe, preserve, and provide long-term access to objects such as technical reports, data, blogs, video recordings of presentations, and web pages. These changes are part of the revolution in scholarly communication—and we are likely to see many more in the next few decades. Academic librarians' roles will be, in part, to keep up with these changes and to explore and create new ways in which libraries remain essential as they continue the time-honored tradition of collecting, preserving, and making available the products of scholarship, learning, and research. In the future, however, those products will not always look like the ones with which we have so long been familiar.

FUTURE RIGHTSIZING

The huge retrospective rightsizing projects undertaken in the early twenty-first century, either individually or in concert with consortial partners, will not be the last such undertakings. Individual libraries should continue periodic evaluation of their physical collections as the items that were once new or moderately well-used travel along their life cycles to become low-use withdrawal candidates, or as the library acquires more perpetual access electronic journal backfiles. As regional and consortial groups tackle print retention issues collectively, each member library will shoulder some responsibility for contributing material to a shared print repository or for retaining selected titles at its own institution as part of a distributed repository arrangement. Regional and national plans to hold print material in light and dark archives will mature to the point where librarians can easily identify and remove low-use material, secure in the knowledge that sufficient backup copies exist. Librarians may match their pre-1923 print and microform holdings against those of large organizations' files of digitized works and withdraw their own holdings in favor of access to the e-versions. It is even possible that copyright laws may change regarding older out-of-print material or orphan works, permitting third-party digitization and universal or low-cost access to these works. It may become economically feasible for publishers to digitize deep backfiles of books to sell as collections or on a title-by-title basis. Print-on-demand services have already moved us into an era when many books will never go out of print when a physical copy is required.

In the same way that librarians cull older and unused titles from their PDA plans, so must they eventually plan to rightsize other portions of their electronic collections. Just because the collections are intangible does not mean that they should continue to grow indefinitely without occasional review. An e-book will, over time, become as obsolete as its print counterpart. In a few years users will face the same difficulty when trying to find a few recent and relevant e-books among dozens of less useful titles in their search results as they do today when browsing unweeded shelves. Or will search algorithms evolve to provide more intuitive results, or will systems be designed to query users to help them create better search statements?

The reasons why librarians today weed print books, to identify older editions, outdated information, and low-use titles, will be equally relevant for weeding e-books. However, weeding e-books may present some new challenges, depending on how the titles were first acquired. Were they part of an e-book package or part of a consortial purchase? Is it possible to suppress selected titles or to delete only a few titles from a larger package? What are best practices for handling these processes? Analyzing past e-book use presents its own challenges because vendors' use statistics provide myriad variables that are often difficult to compare. To suppress or remove a title now, library staff must often contact the vendor to handle each title individually and, even when suppressed, the publisher may still consider these items to be part of the library's licensed content. As with many aspects of rapidly evolving e-books, these challenges may become easier to solve over time, especially if librarians communicate effectively with vendors and publishers regarding desired features and characteristics (Crosetto 2012; Moroni 2012).

The coming decades will doubtless introduce methods we cannot even conceive of today for making the need for most libraries to hold copies of most print books and journals nearly obsolete from the point of view of preserving scholarship. Electronic access will become ubiquitous and user acceptance nearly universal. There will be sufficient fail-safe physical backup copies and many academic libraries will take an active part in preserving this print heritage. Perhaps a formal national plan or network will emerge in the United States for preserving and maintaining legacy print collections, or perhaps the current model of separately administered regional and consortial collaborative collections will persist, although linked by formal or informal cooperative resource-sharing arrangements. Publishers large and small may issue almost all new content in electronic format only, but usually with an option for on-demand print copies should a few be required. Librarians will continue to play a vital role in shaping and maintaining a local collection's content and in selecting which titles to present to users and how to present them. They will also facilitate their patrons' access to the vast wealth of content available in the collective print collections and in the legacy digital archives. In addition, librarians' roles will include collecting, selecting, and digitizing rare and unique material to contribute to the collective collections.

Are these predictions just dreams? If librarians define and embrace a shared vision of the future, these predictions could become reality. Kieft and Payne wrote about "an ideal state for academic library print collections [that] will allow readers and researchers to discover and take full advantage of a universally available, communally preserved, audited library of digitized text and to discover and borrow preserved print materials through consortially funded and governed repository and archiving systems" (Kieft and Payne 2012, 137). Based on the work that many libraries and consortia have already engaged in, librarians are on their way to building this future for their users.

CONCLUSION

In 1954, Walsh concluded his article on selecting library books for storage with the following observation:

> Whoever undertakes to do such selection must expect a certain amount of criticism and must be prepared to change his mind in particular cases.

> It is a work of compromise at best; no librarian likes to send books away
> from his library, and no faculty member likes to see them go. But when
> problems of space make it impossible any longer to put off some pro-
> cess of weeding the library's collections, every effort should be made
> to see that the selection is done in such a way as to cause the least
> inconvenience to the fewest people (Walsh 1954, 381).

Today and in the future, librarians will seldom have the luxury of time, staff,
and other resources to undertake title-by-title deselection in which colleagues
and teaching faculty review endless lists or carts of potential candidates for
withdrawal. Modern methods for creating algorithms based on multiple variables and sophisticated criteria make it possible to produce lists of no- and
low-use books for which partner libraries hold an adequate number copies
and lists of scarce titles that the local library should preserve for the good of
the larger scholarly community. Fast and reliable resource-sharing networks
provide quick access to material that is not held locally, whether or not it
was *ever* held locally. Access to perpetual access electronic journal backfiles
makes maintaining the local equivalent print serial runs redundant overnight.
Local storage of widely held low- and no-use material is no longer the obvious solution for most libraries. Academic libraries of all sizes have joined, or
have access to, formal regional collaborations for at least relatively permanent
and stable print journal repository storage of journal titles. Many consortia
have undertaken similar, distributed collaborations in which members take
responsibility for maintaining one of several (usually two or three) copies of
widely held, but low-use book titles, so that other members may safely discard
theirs. In the years to come, large research libraries with plans to maintain
their print storage facilities for the foreseeable future may formally undertake
to keep and maintain tens or hundreds of thousands of these low-use titles,
provide lists of these titles against which other libraries can make withdrawal
decisions, and continue to allow resource-sharing access, possibly for fees that
are justifiably higher than the national average cost to offset their significant
financial investment in maintaining these collections.

Substantial rightsizing of the local collection indicates that university
administrators and librarians have reached the point where they understand
that their particular library does not have a responsibility to preserve as big
a piece of the cultural record as possible. Rather, the library's responsibility is
to build and continually shape a collection that is useful to its patrons, to facilitate rapid access to material that it does not hold locally, and to contribute or
maintain some portion of the collective cultural record as part of centralized or
distributed print retention agreements with consortial partners. Rightsizing
the physical collection moves the academic library towards presenting a more
"distinctive and institutionally relevant service portfolio" (Malpas 2011, 10).

As a librarian, the author hopes that the physical book will survive in the future, even if only on a limited scale. She hopes it will always be possible to order an on-demand low-cost copy of a novel to tuck into a beach bag, or a special edition of an old favorite to give as a gift, or a beloved classic to put into a child's hands. Surely our archives and museums will continue to preserve printed books of historical and artistic value. But for the majority of academic libraries, the need to retain on-site hundreds of thousands of low-use older print volumes is drawing to a close.

References

Anderson, Chris. 2006. *The Long Tail: Why the Future of Business Is Selling Less of More*. New York: Hyperion.

Ash, Lee Michael. 1963. *Yale's Selective Book Retirement Program*. Hamdon, CT: Archon Books.

Auburn University Libraries. 2011. "Weeding/Discard Procedures." www.lib.auburn .edu/discard/.

Banks, Julie. 2002. "Weeding Book Collections in the Age of the Internet." *Collection Building* 21 (3): 113–19.

Barclay, Donald A. 2010. "The Myth of Browsing." *American Libraries* 41 (6–7): 52–54.

Bazirjian, Rosann. 1990. "The Ethics of Library Discard Practices." *Acquisitions Librarian* 2 (3): 135–46.

Bird, Gwen, and Gohar Ashoughian. 2012. "All Together Now: Planning for Shared Print Archiving at Canada's Western Universities." *Collection Management* 37 (3–4): 260–70.

Borkowski, Casimir, and Murdo J. MacLeod. 1979. "Report on the Kent Study of Library Use: A University of Pittsburgh Reply." *Library Acquisitions* 3 (3–4): 125–51.

Bracke, Marianne Stowell, and Jim Martin. 2005. "Developing Criteria for the Withdrawal of Print Content Available Online." *Collection Building* 24 (2): 61–64.

Bracke, Marianne Stowell, Jean-Pierre V. M. Hérubel, and Suzanne M. Ward. 2010. "Some Thoughts on Opportunities for Collection Development Librarians." *Collection Management* 35 (3–4): 255–59.

Bravender, Patricia, and Valeria Long. 2011. "Weeding an Outdated Collection in an Automated Retrieval System." *Collection Management* 36 (4): 237–45.

Britten, William A. 1990. "A Use Statistic for Collection Management: The 80/20 Rule Revisited." *Library Acquisitions* 14(2): 183–89.

Broadus, Robert N. 1980. "Use Studies of Library Collections." *Library Resources and Technical Services* 24 (4): 317–24.

Brookes, B. C. 1970. "The Growth, Utility and Obsolescence of Scientific Periodical Literature." *Journal of Documentation* 26 (4): 283–94.

Bulick, Stephen, William N. Sabor, and Roger Flynn. 1979. "Circulation and In-House Use of Books." In *Use of Library Materials: The University of Pittsburgh Study,* edited by Allen Kent, Jacob Cohen, K. Leon Montgomery, James G. Williams, Stephen Bulick, Roger R. Flynn, William N. Sabor, and Una Mansfield, 9–55. New York: Marcel Dekker.

Burton, R. E., and Kebler, R. W. 1960. "The Half-Life of Some Science and Technology Literatures." *American Documentation* 11 (1): 18–22.

Clement, Susanne K. 2012. "From Collaborative Purchasing towards Collaborative Discarding: The Evolution of the Shared Print Repository." *Collection Management* 37 (3–4): 153–67.

Cole, P. F. 1963. "Journal Usage vs. Age of Journals." *Journal of Documentation* 19 (1): 1–11.

Colwell, Ernest Cadman. 1949. "Cooperation or Suffocation." *College and Research Libraries* 10 (3, pt. 1): 195–98, 202.

Cooper, Ruth, and David Norris. 2007. "To Bin or Not to Bin? Deselecting Print Back-Runs Available Electronically at Imperial College London Library." *Serials: The Journal for the Serials Community* 20(3): 208–14.

Courant, Paul, and Matthew Nielson. 2010. "On the Cost of Keeping a Book." In *The Idea of Order: Transforming Research Collections for 21st Century Scholarship,* 87–111. Washington, DC: Council on Library and Information Resources.

Crosetto, Alice. 2012. "Weeding E-books." In *No Shelf Required 2,* edited by Sue Polanka, 93–101. Chicago: American Library Association.

Crosetto, Alice, Laura Kinner, and Lucy Duhon. 2008. "Assessment in a Tight Tame Frame: Using Readily Available Data to Evaluate Your Collection." *Collection Management* 33 (1–2): 29–50.

Demas, Sam, and Wendy Lougee. 2011. "Shaping a National Collective Collection: Will Your Campus Participate?" *Library Issues* 31 (6): 1–4.

"Discarding Useless Material." 1911. *New York Libraries* 2 (7): 221–22.

Dubicki, Eleanora. 2008. "Weeding: Facing the Fears." *Collection Building* 17 (4): 132–35.

Eldredge, Jonathan D. 1998. "The Vital Few Meet the Trivial Many: Unexpected Use Patterns in a Monographs Collection." *Bulletin of the Medical Library Association* 86 (4):496–503.

Engeldinger, Eugene A. 1999. "Weeding 'Naturally'." *College and Undergraduate Libraries* 6 (1): 47–50.

Farber, Evan. 1998. "Weeding the Collection: Painful but Necessary." *Library Issues* 19 (2): 1–3.

Fleming, Thomas. P., and Frederick. G. Kilgour. 1964. "Moderately and Heavily Used Biomedical Journals." *Bulletin of the Medical Library Association* 52 (1): 234–41.

Fohl, Claire. 2001. "Weeding: An Experience at Columbus State Community College." *Community and Junior College Libraries* 10 (3):47–50.

Freiburger, Gary. 2010. "A 'White Elephant' in the Library: A Case Study on Loss of Space from the Arizona Health Sciences Library at the University of Arizona." *Journal of the Medical Library Association* 98 (1): 29–31.

Gallagher, Brian T., and Andrée J. Rathemacher. 2012. "Need Exceeds Space: A Serials Withdrawal Project at the University of Rhode Island University Libraries." *Library Resources and Technical Services* 56 (2): 94–103.

Genoni, Paul. 2012. "Storage of Legacy Print Collections: The Views of Australasian University Librarians." *Collection Management* 37 (1): 23–46.

Gore, Daniel. 1976. "Introduction." In *Farewell to Alexandria: Solutions to Space, Growth, and Performance Problems of Libraries,* edited by Daniel Gore, 3–5. Westport, CT: Greenwood Press.

Gosnell, Charles Francis. 1950. "Systematic Weeding." *College and Research Libraries* 11 (2): 137–38.

Handis, Michael W. 2007. "Practical Advice for Weeding in Small Academic Libraries." *Collection Building* 26 (3) 84–88.

Hardesty, Larry. 1981. "Use of Library Materials at a Small Liberal Arts College." *Library Research* 3 (3): 261–82.

Hardin, Garrett. 1947. "The Doctrine of Sufferance in the Library." *College and Research Libraries* 8 (2): 120–24.

Harloe, Bart. 1984. "The Politics of Weeding: New Myths and Old Realities." In *Academic Libraries: Myths and Realities: Proceedings of the Third National Conference of the Association of College and Research Libraries,* edited by Suzanne C. Dodson and Gary L. Menges, 263–68. Chicago: Association of College and Research Libraries.

Harris, C. 1977. "A Comparison of Issues and In-Library Use of Books." *Aslib Proceedings* 29 (3): 118–26.

Haynes, Craig. 2010. "Integrating with Users Is One Thing, but Living with Them? A Case Study on Loss of Space from the Medical Center Library, University of California, San Diego." *Journal of the Medical Library Association* 98 (1): 32–35.

Housewright, Ross. 2010. "A Rock and a Hard Place: Print Collections and Faculty Attitudes." *Against the Grain* 22 (5): 36, 38.

Housewright, Ross, Roger C. Schonfeld, and Kate Wulfson. 2013. *Ithaka S+R US Faculty Survey 2012*. New York: ITHAKA. www.sr.ithaka.org/sites/default/files/reports/Ithaka_SR_US_Faculty_Survey_2012_FINAL.pdf.

Itner, Sheila A. 2006. "Weeding, Collection Development, and Preservation." *Technicalities* 26 (3): 1, 14–18.

Kelley, Michael. 2013. "Don't Judge a Book by Its Dust." *Library Journal* 138 (2): 8.

Kieft, Robert H., and Lizanne Payne. 2012. "Collective Collection, Collective Action." *Collection Management* 37 (3–4): 137–52.

Kyrillidou, Martha, Shaneka Morris, and Gary Roebuck. 2012. *ARL Statistics 2010–2011*. Washington, DC: Association of Research Libraries. http://publications.arl.org/ARL-Statistics-2010-2011.

Lee, Hur-Li. 1993. "The Library Space Problem, Future Demand, and Collection Control." *Library Resources and Technical Services* 37 (2): 147–66.

Line, Maurice B. 1970. "The 'Half-Life' of Periodical Literature: Apparent and Real Obsolescence." *Journal of Documentation* 26 (1): 46–54.

Little, Geoffrey. 2013. "The Space Race." *Journal of Academic Librarianship* 39 (4): 351–353.

Lucker, Kay K., Kate S. Herzog, and Sydney J. Owens. 1986. "Weeding Collections in an Academic Library System." *Science and Technology Libraries* 6 (3): 11–23.

Lugg, Rick, and Ruth Fischer. 2008a. "The Disapproval Plan: Rules-Based Weeding and Storage Decisions." *Against the Grain* 20 (6): 74–76.

Lugg, Rick, and Ruth Fischer. 2008b. "Weeding: The Time Is Now." *Against the Grain* 20 (4): 87–88.

Lugg, Rick, and Ruth Fischer. 2009. "Doing What's Obvious: Library Space and the Fat Smoker." *Against the Grain* 21 (1): 75–76.

Malpas, Constance. 2011. *Cloud-Sourcing Research Collections: Managing Print in the Mass-Digitized Library Environment*. Dublin, OH: OCLC Research. www.oclc.org/content/dam/research/publications/library/2011/2011–01.pdf?urlm=162949.

Malpas, Constance, and Brian Lavoie. 2014. *Right-Scaling Stewardship: A Multi-Scale Perspective on Cooperative Print Management*. Dublin, OH: OCLC Research. http://oclc.org/content/dam/research/publications/library/2014/oclcresearch-cooperativeprint-management-2014.pdf.

Manley, Will. 2003. "Readers Need Weeders." *American Libraries* 34 (10): 80.

Manley, Will. 2014. "Treasure or Trash Heap?" *American Libraries* 45 (1–2): 80.

Marcum, James W. 2008. "Books as Inventory: Suggested Lessons from Business." *The Bottom Line: Managing Library Finances* 21 (1): 14–16.

Martin, Jess A., and Steven B. Manch. 1971. "Library Weeds." *Bulletin of the Medical Library Association* 59 (4): 599–602.

McCarthy, J. P. 2007. "Some Thoughts on Legacy Collections." *Library Management* 28 (6–7): 347–54.

McGaw, Howard F. 1956. "Policies and Practices in Discarding." *Library Trends* 4 (3): 269–82.

Metz, Paul, and Caryl Gray. 2005. "Public Relations and Library Weeding." *Journal of Academic Librarianship* 31 (3): 273–79.

Moroni, Alene E. 2012. "Weeding in a Digital Age: Shelf Clutter Can Be a Problem for Ebooks as Well." *Library Journal* 137 (15): 26–28.

Nixon, Judith M., and E. Stewart Saunders. 2010. "A Study of Circulation Statistics of Books on Demand: A Decade of Patron-Driven Collection Development." *Collection Management* 35 (3–4): 151–61.

Northeastern State University Libraries. 2014. "Weeding Policy." library.nsuok.edu/reference/weedingpol.html.

Persily, Gail L., and Karen A. Butter. 2010. "Reinvisioning and Redesigning 'A Library for the Fifteenth through Twenty-First Centuries': A Case Study on Loss of Space from the Library and Center for Knowledge Management, University of California, San Francisco." *Journal of the Medical Library Association* 98 (1): 44–48.

Pidgeon, Alice. 1995. "On Writing a Deselection Policy; or, How to Toss Books without Public Condemnation." *Against the Grain* 7: 68–69, 86.

Ramirez, Debbie A. 2013. "Weeding Lessons." *Library Journal* 138 (4): 10.

Reed, Lawrence L., and Rodney Erickson. 1993. "Weeding: A Quantitative and Qualitative Approach." *Library Acquisitions* 17 (2): 175–81.

Reilly, Bernard F., Jr. 2005. "Preserving American Print Resources." *Library Management* 26 (1–2): 102–5.

Report of the Collection Development Executive Committee Task Force on Print Circulation Usage Cornell University Library. 2010. http://staffweb.library.cornell.edu/system/files/CollectionUsageTF_ReportFina111-22-10.pdf.

Reusch, Rita. 1990. "Weeding the Treatise Collection at the University of Utah College Law Library." *Trends in Law Library Management and Technology* 3 (7): 1–2.

"Ridding Collections of Deadwood." 1989. *Journal of Academic Librarianship* 15 (1): 3.

Rogers, Rutherford D. 1950. "Regional Depository Libraries and the Problem of Optimum Size of College and University Libraries." *College and Research Libraries* 11 (2): 147–49.

Roy, Loriene. 1990. "Weeding without Tears." *Collection Management* 12 (1): 83–93.

Roy, Loriene. 1994. "Weeding." In *Encyclopedia of Library and Information Science* edited by Allen Kent, 54 (supplement 17): 352–98. New York: M. Dekker.

Sandison, A. 1971. "The Use and Obsolescence of Older Literature in Libraries." *Journal of Documentation* 27 (3): 184–99.

Sands, John L. 1991. "CD-ROM Destruction (Intentional!): What to Do with Out of Date Disks." *CD-ROM Professional* 4 (2): 58–59.

Sargent, Seymour H. 1979. "The Uses and Limitations of Trueswell." *College and Research Libraries* 40 (5): 416–23.

Scherlen, Allan. 2004. "Courage of Our Convictions: Making Difficult Decisions about Serial Collections." *Serials Review* 30 (2): 117–21.

Schonfeld, Roger C. 2011. "What to Withdraw? Print Collection Management in the Wake of Digitization." *Serials Librarian* 60 (1–4): 141–45.

Schonfeld, Roger C., and Ross Housewright. 2009. *What to Withdraw? Print Collections Management in the Wake of Digitization.* New York: Ithaka S+R. www.sr.ithaka .org/sites/default/files/reports/What_to_Withdraw_Print_Collections _Management_in_the_Wake_of_Digitization.pdf.

Segal, Judith A. 1986. "Journal Deselection: A Literature Review and an Application." *Science and Technology Libraries* 6 (3): 25–42.

Seymour, Carol A. 1972a. "Weeding the Collection: A Review of Research on Identifying Obsolete Stock. Part 1: Monographs." *Libri* 22 (2): 137–48.

Seymour, Carol A. 1972b. "Weeding the Collection: A Review of Research on Identifying Obsolete Stock. Part 2: Serials." *Libri* 22 (3): 183–89.

Slote, Stanley J. 1997. *Weeding Library Collections: Library Weeding Methods.* Englewood, CO: Libraries Unlimited.

Soma, Amy K., and Lisa M. Sjoberg. 2011. "More Than Just Low-Hanging Fruit: A Collaborative Approach to Weeding in Academic Libraries." *Collection Management* 36 (1): 17–28.

Sorensen, Charlene. 2009. "The 5K Run Toolkit: A Quick, Painless, and Thoughtful Approach to Managing Print Journal Backruns." *Serials Review* 35 (4): 228–34.

Stankus, Tony. 1986. "Journal Weeding in Relation to Declining Faculty Member Publishing." *Science and Technology Libraries* 6 (3): 43–53.

Steele, Kirstin. 2011. "Free Electronic Books and Weeding." *The Bottom Line: Managing Library Finances* 24 (3): 160–61.

Stewart, Christopher. 2011. "The Next Chapter: Measuring the Pace of Change for Print Monograph Collections." *Journal of Academic Librarianship* 37 (4): 355–57.

Stockard, Joan, Mary Ann Griffin, and Clementine Coblyn. 1979. "Document Exposure Counts in Three Academic Libraries: Circulation and In-Library Use." In *Quantitative Measurement and Dynamic Library Service,* edited by Ching-Chih Chen, 136–47. Phoenix: Oryx Press.

Stueart, Robert D. 1985. "Weeding of Library Material: Politics and Policies." *Collection Management* 7 (2): 47–58.

Taylor, Colin R. 1976. "A Practical Solution to Weeding University Library Periodicals Collections." *Collection Management* 1 (3–4): 27–46.

Thibodeau, Patricia L. 2010. "When the Library Is Located in Prime Real Estate: A Case Study on the Loss of Space from the Duke University Medical Center Library and Archives." *Journal of the Medical Library Association* 98 (1): 25–28.

Thomas, William Joseph. 2011. "Trusting Digital Preservation for Print Collection Management, or How Librarians Should Learn to Stop Worrying and Love the 'E.'" *Against the Grain* 23 (4): 24–28.

Thomas, William Joseph, and Daniel L. Shouse. 2012. "Rules of Thumb for Deselecting, Relocating, and Retaining Bound Journals." *Collection Building* 31 (3): 92–97.

Tobia, Rajia C. 2002. "Comprehensive Weeding of an Academic Health Sciences Collection: The Briscoe Library Experience." *Journal of the Medical Library Association* 90 (1): 94–98.

Tobia, Rajia C., and Jonquil D. Feldman. 2010. "Making Lemonade from Lemons: A Case Study on Loss of Space at the Dolph Briscoe, Jr. Library, University of Texas Health Science Center at San Antonio." *Journal of the Medical Library Association* 98 (1): 36–39.

Tooey, Mary Joan. 2010. "Renovated, Repurposed, and Still "One Sweet Library:" A Case Study on Loss of Space from the Health Sciences and Human Services Library, University of Maryland, Baltimore." *Journal of the Medical Library Association* 98 (1): 40–43.

Trueswell, Richard W. 1965. "A Quantitative Measure of User Circulation Requirements and Its Possible Effect on Stack Thinning and Multiple Copy Determination." *American Documentation* 16 (1): 20–25.

Trueswell, Richard W. 1969. "Some Behavior Patterns of Library Users: The 80/20 Rule." *Wilson Library Bulletin* 43 (5): 458–61.

Trueswell, Richard. 1976. "Growing Libraries: Who Needs Them? A Statistical Basis for the No-Growth Collection." In *Farewell to Alexandria: Solutions to Space, Growth, and Performance Problems of Libraries,* edited by Daniel Gore, 73–104. Westport, CT: Greenwood Press.

Tyler, David C., Yang Xu, Joyce C. Melvin, MaryLou Epp, and Anita M. Kreps. 2010. "Just How Right Are the Customers? An Analysis of the Relative Performance of Patron-Initiated Interlibrary Loan Monograph Purchases." *Collection Management* 35 (3–4): 162–70.

Voigt, Melvin. J. 1979. "Circulation Studies Cannot Reflect Research Use." *Journal of Academic Librarianship* 5 (2): 66.

Walsh, James E. 1954. "An Experiment in the Selection of Library Books for Storage." *Harvard University Bulletin* 8: 378–81.

Ward, Suzanne M., and Mary C. Aagard. 2008. "The Dark Side of Collection Management: Deselecting Serials from a Research Library's Storage Facility Using WorldCat Collection Analysis." *Collection Management* 33 (4): 272–87.

Webb, Helmer. 1950. "The Optimum Size of the College Library." *College and Research Libraries* 11 (2): 143–47.

Wezeman, Frederick. 1958. "Psychological Barriers to Weeding." *ALA Bulletin* 52 (8): 637–39.

Williams, Roy. 1988. "Choosing the Slote Method of Weeding Library Collections." In *Collection Development: Options for Effective Management: Proceedings of a Conference of the Library and Information Research Group, University of Sheffield, 1987,* edited by Sheila Corrall, 88–94. London: Taylor Graham.

Index

f denotes figures